TEACHING TEACHERS FOR A KNOWLEDGE SOCIETY

TEACHING TEACHERS FOR A KNOWLEDGE SOCIETY

R.P. SINGH

GYAN PUBLISHING HOUSE
NEW DELHI-110002

Teaching Teachers for a Knowledge Society

Rs.690

ISBN: 978-81-212-1005-8

Published in 2008 in India by
Gyan Publishing House
5, Ansari Road, Darya Ganj,
New Delhi-110002
Phones : 23282060, 23261060
Fax : 011-23285914
E-mail: books@gyanbooks.com
Website: www.gyanbooks.com

Laser Type Setting by: Rudra Computer Graphics, Delhi
Printed at : Singhal Print Media, Delhi

Contents

SECTION III

SECTION IV

Preface

The present book is a contribution to the writing on the emerging Knowledge Society in India. Since a society can be maximally impacted via education therefore it is in the fitness of things that we discussed all concepts against the backdrop of the type of changes we envisage will have to be brought about in the field of teacher education, We all know and also believe teacher is the major force behind the greatness of any society and that is why the Vedas too pray that their teachers should be learned and good guides. Read for instance the following prayer.

"A teacher should have the ability to build up the students under his charge. He must never be proud of his knowledge. He should be as glorious as fire and possess qualities of leadership. He must be specialist of his branch of knowledge. Just as a cow collects milk in her udders after grazing grass, a teacher should collect knowledge through reflection and self-study. He should make teaching an enjoyable experience even as food items are made tasty and palatable before they are served. He should be popular among his students and be their benefactor. Sitting in the midst of his students he must look distinguished because of his knowledge" **RIGVEDA** 1/69/2

In the past couple of years the term 'Knowledge Society' has come to be used most commonly for trying to show that our societies differ markedly from the past and that it is for the first time that such a society is about to come into being. On the very face of it, it is not possible to defend the proposition. The fact is that ancient societies were as knowledgeable as us, if not more. In fact in certain senses they had far superior and sophisticated knowledge than what we have today. Look at the Egyptians or the Greeks or for that matter the Chinese they did not lack knowledge and knew also how to use it. Try as we might it is not possible either to match Plato, Aristotle, Confucius or Socrates either for their knowledge or their levels of sagacity. They can put to shame any university professor of our times. It is perhaps because of this fact that the NKC has given some role to traditional knowledge I the upcoming Knowledge Societies.

The only difference in the past societies and the present ones is that while they were elitists and the modern societies are by and large egalitarian. The ancients believed more in intuition and reflection rather than innovations and comforts. That is why while their artifacts can be excelled but seldom their ideas. While Aristotle's theory of Golden Mean; or Plato's Republic is difficult to excel but their contemporary artifacts can. it could be because of this reality a role has been fixed for the traditional knowledge even in the contemporary Knowledge Societies.

The marked differences between the modern and the ancient societies is noticeable in the spread of knowledge in the classes that were until recently debarred from acquiring knowledge. Education is getting to become mass oriented and culture mass based. The other change is in the area information and communication technology. In fact it is the arrival of ICT that has brought about a sea-change in the acceptance of the democratic principles more than any other period in the history of Mankind. The revolution that has engulfed us all is the newly awakened concept and practice of democracy. That is why The End of History is near and the days of settling disputes via wars have few takers.

We want teachers who are both imaginative and also innovative. These things are possible only in democracies. A new kind fresh breeze has started blowing. We all wait for the times when all knowledge will be available to all and when we shall overcome all types of discrimination. For this a need breed of teacher is expected to take birth. We hope the Knowledge Society will offer us that privilege. That is why we have offered the readers a chance to appreciate the difficulties one will have to face. Besides institutional bottlenecks and the bureaucratic hurdles teachers will have to discover both élan and courage to overcome their own tendencies to resist change.

We have a bright future therefore let us hope we discover means to match our efforts.

R.P. Singh

List of Contributors

1. R.P. Singh formerly with the NCERT.
2. S.P. Singh Professor of Biology, Newman University, Wichita, USA.
3. Andrew Tadie, Associate Professor of English, Department of English, Seattle University, USA.
4. Don Hufford, Professor, Newman University, Wichita, USA.
5. Nidhi Saxena, D/ 644 Kamla Nagar, Agra, 4.
6. Rajendra Mishra, Research Scientist, CEC, Aruna Asaf Ali Road, New Delhi.
7. C.P.S. Chauhan; Chairman, Department of Education, Aligarh Muslim University, Aligarh.
8. Dr. Jitendra Sharma, Lecturer, S.G.K.Teachers College, (C.T.E.) Jodhpur.

Introduction: The Context

(Wake up Call)

It is a two part discussion of the New Curriculum

Part 1

The New Curriculum—-THE CONTEXTUAL PERSPECTIVE

R.P. Singh

"We are today at the convergence of nano, bio and information technologies. This age, I feel, will create a historic revolution and we must be in the driver's seat to contribute towards this societal change." President A.P.J. Abdul Kalam (August 1, 2004)

In a globalized, competitive world the cutting edge to the progress of a Nation can be provided only through its classrooms. After all, education is a planned endeavor. Today no nation can afford to neglect the education of its citizenry. Logically enough one has therefore to pay good deal of attention to the preparation of teachers— the dominant players in the classrooms.

All nations like all humans desire to stay competitive and healthy. India is no exception. For predictable reasons these abilities do not come effortlessly. The path to achieving this dream lies through classrooms. In simple terms it is the teacher who eventually sets educational standards for the nation and helps it to attain the same. In the early 50's Professor R.M. Hutchins talked of making the USA an 'Information Society' and on the eve of the third millennium President of India. A.P.J. Abdul Kalam has set for this country the goal of becoming a Knowledge Society. The Government of India has recently set up a Knowledge Commission as well. Without loosing time, the Commission has in the meanwhile made several far-reaching recommendations and also approved six centers where a two-year program B.Ed. has started already. Looks like, without much preparation India has imperceptibly entered the Age of Knowledge.

What exactly is the definition of Knowledge Society? How does it differ from all other societies? What is needed to make India achieve this goal? What are the types of teachers that a Knowledge Society needs? The obvious next question is: What structures and organizations are needed to have adequate number of qualified teachers for such a society? These are a few of the many questions that need answers before one is able to identify oneself with the efforts to achieving this goal.

The Nature of a Knowledge Society

Knowledge societies are the societies of shared knowledge. The concept of knowledge society is an improvement on the concept of information society. Information is only a small part of the knowledge. Universal access to knowledge is the pillar that supports the transition from information societies to knowledge societies. A knowledge society does not replace all of its earlier knowledge with recent knowledge. In fact, it filters the past knowledge and retains that which is still valid and can be used by the modern tools of knowledge. Internet and other modern tools cannot throw away the traditional tools of textbooks, story telling, etc. In spite of the availability of self-learning opportunities, the role of teachers will continue to have its place even in the next millennium. Expansion of knowledge societies is indispensable for the reduction of poverty, the implementation of collective security and the effective exercise of human rights. Knowledge societies are nurtured by diversity and capacities. They are acknowledged by characteristics such as freedom of opinion and expression (Article 19 of the Universal Declaration of Human Rights) as well as freedom of information, media pluralism and academic freedom, the right to education and its corollary, free basic education and progress towards free access to other levels of education (Article 26 of the Universal Declaration of Human Rights and Article 13 of the International Covenant on Economic, Social and Cultural Rights); and the right to "freely participate in the cultural life of the community, to enjoy the arts and to share in scientific advancement and its benefits" (Article 27, paragraph 1, of the Universal Declaration of Human Rights).

Knowledge societies are also characterized by profuse utilization of information communication technology in the form of Internet, mobile telephony and digital technologies that create new opportunities for development.

Curriculum Framework for a Knowledge Society

The relevance of it all should be seen against the backdrop of the arrangements that a government has to make in order to usher in societal changes without pain. In terms of education not only there has to be equal access to education for all but also high quality education should be made available to all. Efforts have to be made for an education "study time entitlement" that would entitle people to a certain number of years of education after the completion of compulsory schooling, usable by all depending on their personal choices, paths, experience and timetables. Knowledge societies have their foundation on a "double multilingualism"- that of individuals and that of cyberspace. Hence, it is essential that multilingualism is encouraged. Students have the capacity to learn many languages. The knowledge society requires teachers to be trained in skills of facilitating lifelong education skills among their students. They need also to be trained in accessing quality materials available on the Internet. It must be ensured that the materials available on Internet are reliable, their contents relevant, especially in the area of scientific information. Without appropriate guidance, the students will unnecessarily spend a lot of time without achieving any purpose.

The present curriculum framework is a continuation and part of the efforts that have been made in the past couple of decades or more. Normally, curricular frameworks provide guidance for the formulation of courses of study for various examinations. Details of curricular transaction vary from one provider of teacher training to another depending on various factors such as abilities of teacher trainees, abilities of teacher educators, availability of relevant human and material resources, etc. In 1978, the first curriculum for teacher education was brought out by NCERT for its NCTE. It was followed by a model curriculum developed by the UGC Curriculum Development Centre in Education at the University of Kerala. The second one was brought out in 1988. After NCTE became a statutory body, it brought out in 1998 a Curriculum Framework. In 2004, NCERT made an effort to bring out a Curriculum Framework for Teacher Education. In 2005, NCTE brought out a Draft Curriculum Framework but it had limited circulation. In 2006, another Draft for Discussion on Curriculum Framework was developed by the NCTE in collaboration with NCERT. This was put on the website of NCTE for discussion.

But even before the discussion on the latest framework was completed the present group, chaired by me was constituted to look at the changed scenario. Curriculum frameworks provide guidance for the formulation of courses of study for various examinations. The NCTE has thought it fit to remain in step with the current mood of the government to be ready with a *Curriculum Framework for a Knowledge Society.* Also, a few major social and pedagogical concerns have come to constitute the NCTE agenda that need to be paid immediate attention. And lastly, our teachers could easily become our social and economic ambassadors, if they attract the attention of the employers abroad. In fact, EU has recently come to note that Indians are the most highly qualified immigrant population in Europe. After ICT, our teachers abroad could shore up our intellectual reputation even further. Obviously this area opens up an opportunity to prepare teachers for advanced countries.

The present teacher curriculum framework is based on following factors:

1. Theoretical base for professional knowledge and understanding .
2. Professional reflection on educational processes in a wide variety of contexts that promote professional values and personal commitment and a range of qualities including intellectual independence and rationality.
3. Activities in individualized and group settings that develop professional skills and abilities such as (a) ability to construct and sustain a reasoned argument about educational issues in a clear, lucid and coherent manner; and (b) Skills of teaching and other related work.
4. Partnership with a variety of schools and other agencies to provide experiences of a wide range of strategies of teaching.
5. Effective use of ICT to facilitate learning and teaching.

6. Promoting mobility and co-operation.
7. Encouraging intercultural respect and understanding.
8. Working effectively with the local community, and with partners and stakeholders in education – parents, teacher education institutions, and representative groups.

National Policies and the Curricular Framework

The National Policy on Education 1986 stated that "Teacher education is a continuous process and its pre-service and in-service components are inseparable. As the first step, the system of teacher education will be overhauled" It was stated that teacher education programmes will emphasize continuing education. All aspirants for teachers' jobs need not only knowledge of pedagogy and value orientation but also certain skills essential for teaching. Schools are the crucial players in all types of societies. The quality of teachers determines the quality of the school. The values of teachers in a school system leave a deep impression on the students. The behaviour, attitudes, relationships with and interest in pupils of teachers mould not only learning styles but also personality styles of students. Teachers play a crucial role in the development of nations. Effective initial teacher education programmes are professionally demanding.

Teachers and Their Roles

Developments in science and technology have been instrumental in the development of new ideas and technologies that can be used by teachers. This makes it imperative to continuously update both the initial as well as in-service teacher training. The learning process can never come to an end. Teacher's quality is a point of concern the world over. Teacher's task is becoming increasing difficult as it is one such social practice that is dominated by social and moral complexities, all round uncertainties and even conflicts of values. An effective teacher therefore is an intellectual transformer.

Teaching

Researches point out that there are variety of ways of teaching a topic, depending on the capacity of the teacher and students and resources available for the purpose. Effective teaching lays stress on building student's ability to learn independently. It also builds the skill for carrying out learning as a lifelong pursuit. Every teacher needs to acquire adequate knowledge about pedagogy. The knowledge of pedagogy involves high quality questioning and feedback, guidance and other help offered by teachers to students. An 'effective' teacher considers using ideas suggested by students in developing a lesson. The intellectual and social climate created by the teachers influences the level of students' learning. 'Effective teaching' involves taking efficient decisions on the method of teaching, the resources to be used, the key ideas and skills that are to be covered and the mechanism of teacher evaluation of learning of students.

Teaching Profession

Teaching as a profession is relatively more strenuous than other professions. Teachers throughout the world seem to be under stress. The state of teachers' mental health is an essential factor that determines his/her effectiveness as a teacher. A teacher may be highly qualified and experienced but if s/he does not keep good mental health doing justice to his/ her job will remain an unfulfilled dream. The teacher of the present century is not only a manager of classroom activities but a manager of community welfare activities as well. A good classroom teacher works continuously during his/ her working hours, either physically or mentally. The working hours of the schools are the only hours during which the teacher implements the plan of action that had been formulated outside school working hours. This consumes time. Good teachers are therefore always overworked. Even so teachers the world over suffer from factors like low pay, high risks, lower status resulting in low morale, etc. Teaching profession requires persons who have appropriate aptitude for teaching. Proper ways have to be evolved to regulate the practice of giving private tuitions and coaching classes.

Teacher Effectiveness

Teacher effectiveness refers to the expertise of teachers in promoting learning of the students. Researches fail to define 'effectiveness' conclusively. In earlier days, an effective teacher was the one who had mastery over theologically-based knowledge. After the Renaissance, the definition of knowledge itself underwent a change. Today we are offering guidance to students to learn and select information techniques to master knowledge Teachers encourage students to use active techniques (experiments, real-world problem-solving) to create more knowledge and then to reflect on and talk about what they are doing and how their understanding is changing. The teacher makes sure s/he understands the students' pre-existing conceptions, and guides the activity to address them and then build on them. But all these variables result in teacher's mastery over content and command on communication skills.

Aims of Education

The aims of education vary from nation to nation. For our purpose we have borrowed them from a NCERT Report. According to that committee education is a deliberate intervention in the life of a child. In other words, the said intervention is defined and qualified by the society. Education being a continuous process the child needs to be so taught that teaching results in a virtuous behaviour. It needs mentioning that all virtues do not always result in a good, ethical behavior. For instance, courage is needed both by a soldier staking his life for killing his Nation's enemy and also by a criminal for killing an innocent man. One must acquire virtue only for the social good. Let us acknowledge that India is culturally diverse, where knowledge is to be acquired for getting liberated from the shackles of injustices such as gender biases, the menace of caste discrimination, poverty etc. besides all kind of exploitation of one by the other. These being the goals of education, they should get reflected in the school curricula as well as in the preparation of teachers.

As it is, we have in the country several modes of preparing teachers. For instance, we have the Distance mode, one year face – to –face B.Ed, the 4 year integrated course and also an experimental two-year model. The agencies involved in teacher preparation range from the central government to the local municipalities. Of late, private funded teacher education programs have come to dominate the entire scenario. There is nothing amiss with the private-aided colleges in the area of teacher education. The truth is that in most countries the private-financed colleges and even universities command greater respect than the government –funded or supported institutions.

Several State universities in the meantime too have discovered the potential of B.Ed. degree for minting money on the sidelines. A few have gone on to earn notoriety in this area because of the (active?) typical academic liberality of the UGC. Although it is hard to agree that universities in India have the autonomy like their Oxbridge counterparts, they continue to flaunt it as a banner in the void when the selfish interests of a few State officials and the universities converge. There is every reason to believe that a separate management system has to be created to look after the mushrooming of privately-financed colleges as it is unwise to expect them to be easily regulated at this stage. These colleges unfortunately carry the stigma of having 'commercialized' teacher education, which the Report of the Education Commission (1964-66) had squarely condemned. The dubious roles of a large number of the present day professorial class cannot be easily overlooked in all this. They did not cover themselves with any glory for having compromised their personal ethics along with the honor of the apex body in approving colleges that produce 'unemployable' teachers. The quality of teaching is a key determinant of student learning. It depends on the quality of the people in the teaching profession, their initial teacher education and their continuing professional development, as well as their work practices and working environment. Teachers constitute the largest component of education expenditure. It is in this perspective that a nation must think of teacher preparation.

In terms of teacher training the quality of knowledge invariably gets defined by the type of institution and its staff; besides, the operant conditionalities. While it is possible to upgrade the physical conditions and quality of an institution but the quality of its intellectual ambience and freedom require much more than mere library, equipment and similar other inputs. As it is, we can see these knowledge boundaries and the quality of institutions getting defined by the class patronage and their resultant ambience. If knowledge begets power, the power lays down its own boundaries. Despite all that has happened, the institutional quality is stamped on the quality of its product. Under the circumstances, it is totally unjust to define products in terms of their legally-approved paper certificates.

The present curriculum frame hopes to offer an acceptable resolution to the cantankerous problems the NCTE faces today. It is advisable for policy makers to read books like the one Arthur Levine has brought out in September 2006 titled *Educating School Teachers* (*Teacher Education Project),* which talks of the American Teacher Education program *as the pursuit of irrelevance.* He finds the present-day American teacher education curricula in a state of disarray. While the American standards of education are low, the quality control insufficient, the curriculum makes for inadequate preparation of teachers and the faculty remains highly disconnected. Based on a massive research data the report records "the inescapable conclusion is that the nation's teacher education programs are not adequately preparing their students." (p. 33). It is an important question that demands an answer. Do we in India find ourselves in a better state?

Perhaps here we might as well define the job of the class-teacher:

1. S/he should have a sound understanding of the standards of student learning.
2. S/he should design appropriate and effective learning units. Standards need to be defined in terms of factual, conceptual and procedural knowledge.
3. Teachers must be aware of the need for curricular alignment such as connection between the standards/ objectives, the assessments, and the instructional activities.

The NCTE has to improve the quality of school teachers, teacher educators and also of the delivery mechanism alongside. The NCTE must address a few commitments made by the Government in the two Houses of Parliament and these are:

1. The B.Ed. program should cover comprehensive, systematic, scientific approaches of Health Education and Health care and consider already developed curricula for improving the quality of education in this field. While doing so the work done both by the WHO and the UNICEF may also be closely followed.
2. The new curriculum should seriously consider and reflect disability component keeping in view the Human Rights perspective. The needs of Special Children as covered in

the Comprehensive National Action Plan may be included at the appropriate place in the existing Health Education paper at the B.Ed. level.

3. The problems and the issues concerning the Education of the minorities as recounted in the Sachchar Committee Report have also to be addressed.
4. Consider promotion of corporate institutional life based on values and ideals enshrined in the Indian Constitution among all stakeholders.
5. To reconsider issues related to promoting ICT as an integral part of teacher education and improving the quality of teacher education by giving more time to practice teaching than currently being given.
6. Consider upgrading teacher education program suited for a Knowledge Society.
7. Suggesting a plan of action for involving CTEs, IASEs and DIETs for playing a greater role in the in-service education of the school teachers and the teacher educators.
8. Considering environment education as part of school-teachers curriculum. Specialization in this area may be considered at the M.Ed levels.
9. Lack of awareness among teachers about the government's policies of education.

Therefore, it is high time we changed our track in this connection. We should not overlook the fact that our educational system is getting increasingly exposed to the onslaught of foreign institutions. Our teachers have to be equipped to face this challenge. The curriculum for the teacher education should change drastically.

We have to think also of developing language and communication skills; skills in reasoning and logic more especially lateral thinking; disabuse the minds of teachers against prejudices, define a prejudice—racial, caste, color, language, sex etc and discuss techniques of eradicating the same; and in the process teach meaning of life and how to develop a philosophy of life and replace totally schools of philosophy; and lastly, teach classroom management and ideal behavior and not theories or models of teaching This is only an example. The main principle to be observed is: Teach nothing that is either irrelevant or is a mere theory. Teaching to learn is always superior to teaching to store. Therefore, improve the process and aim at quality production.

Whether or not we should have norms is a question that needs an unequivocal answer.

While having norms continues to be a cherished ideal but their enforcement is likely to remain a major ticklish issue for a long time to come. It is a quiz without a definable clue.

Part 2

TEACHER LICENSING TEST IN INDIA

"We wish our Guru to possess highly specialized knowledge that is as dear to us as life itself and which could be acquired through harmless activities. We want him to have knowledge of sciences, speak cultivated tongue, know the meaning of the Sastras (Researches), reflect deeply… and thereby be a highly competent and knowledgeable teacher." Yajurveda 36/ 16

Rationale for Introducing a Teacher Licensing Test

While preparing teachers we have to think of giving them a competitive edge in the world economy. According to the contemporary history the Vision for India's higher education and the professionals has come from the President of India himself who has been trying to persuade Indians to accept that the *Vision is to become a Knowledge Society* and *the time-frame for this is the year 2020.* In the hope that something concrete might emerge out of this Vision a Knowledge Commission too has been set up to perform the Mission with well-defined goals. It would be a pleasant surprise if these dreams become a reality. Our recommendation is merely a step in that direction.

The principal reason for introducing teacher licensing system, however, is that there exists no parity in the degrees and diplomas being awarded in the country at the same time all teacher education degrees and diplomas, irrespective of the location and the affiliating university, today legally and technically stand at par with each other. Neither the conditions of admission nor the department or the university counts for much when a teacher is being selected. It is only the certificate that validates the appointment. It should in fact be a matter of concern when candidates are equated merely by the degrees (on paper) and not on the basis of institutions or by the type of courses they may have opted for. Teacher licensing will ensure that the degrees certify standardization in the quality of the product.

The disparate quality of products (whether real or imaginary) has to be homogenized and the school system should be offered the best of the choice. Since it is neither necessary nor possible to close down any institution the only alternative we have is to propose the creation of a system like the NET called *National Teachers Competencies Test* with certificates specifying grades: one, for the schoolteachers and *the other* for Teacher Educators. One could think of replicating the same at the State level too.

The test content may include items that reflect on traits such as personality of the teacher; emotional quotient, intelligence, thinking / reasoning skills, aptitude and general awareness of the nature of society.

This Test once introduced would enable teacher education system to become more regulated and standardized than what it is today. This would help the NCTE to acquire its legitimate status i.e. of being an Apex body. This single recommendation, if implemented, would bring about considerable improvement in the present scenario.

The creation of sub-standard teacher education institutions is totally unacceptable. As the system advances the quality of schools must be able to ensure quality. No civilized society can survive for long if it fails to ensure that its citizens receive quality education.

Therefore not unlike most of the developed countries that have a teacher licensing system based on a performance test after a candidate obtains a qualification in teacher training and has been through a period of mentoring under the guidance of an expert school teacher, *a system of teacher licensing is being proposed for India as well.* Institutions like Navodaya Vidyalayas, which admit only talented students, face an extreme shortage of competent teachers. For these types of schools advanced level training is urgently needed. Logically enough they need advanced level screening too that may necessitate creation of Advanced Level posts of Teachers at various stages of education. In brief, *the system being proposed is to standardize employability conditions that will provide equivalence in the degrees irrespective of the mode and the place / institution from where ever one might come.* It would eventually standardize teacher education competencies and skills and put an end to the present day prevailing conditions.

In almost all branches of employment we notice that the candidate who comes for a job has to undergo some kind of test—whether written or otherwise. Then there are placement agencies that grade institutions and look for the best candidates. We have in the teacher education area neither graded institutions nor any external agency trying to grade candidates. The licensing system being proposed would fill in the lacuna.

Tests for Issue of Provisional License

This test shall measure knowledge of specific subjects that a teacher candidate will opt to teach, as well as general and subject-specific teaching skills and relevant information. There shall be three sections: 1. Content Knowledge Test; 2. General Knowledge and Skills Test; 3. Subject-specific Teaching Knowledge and Skills Test. There shall be both multiple-choice and constructed-response test items. The content knowledge level for provisional license for teaching (a) at pre-school level and at elementary school level in the classes I to V, shall be higher secondary level content in subjects taught at this stage, such as: Mother tongue, English/Hindi, Mathematics, General Science, Social Studies. In the case of teaching of classes VI-VIII of Elementary school level the qualifications shall be as laid down in collaboration with the department of education of Delhi University. The NCTE is however free to choose some other university for its collaboration. The system or the choices shall remain open to revision and review by the NCTE. And for classes IX-X the content knowledge test will be of degree level and will cover two subjects In case of classes XI and XII, there shall be one subject of PG level. General Knowledge and Skills Test and Subject-specific Teaching Knowledge and Skills Test shall use Case Study approach and shall consist of constructed-response and multiple-choice items.

Test for Issue of General License for Teaching

This test shall have two sections: 1. Classroom Teaching Skill Test; and 2. Review of documentation prepared by the candidate. Classroom Teaching Skill Test shall have three stages: *Pre-observation Interview*, *Classroom Observation* and *Post-observation interview.* The assessor will include one Inspector/Supervisor of Schools, the head of the institution and the Mentor. Review of the documentation prepared by the candidate shall be undertaken by one faculty member, teaching initial teacher training course of that level, one Inspector/ Supervisor of Schools and the head of the institution, where the candidate had taken the training.

It is here that we propose a role for the IASEs, SCERTs, DIETs and the CTEs under the guidance of NCTE. This is one stage / area, where the mettle of these institutions shall get tested.

Test for Issue of Advanced License for Teaching

The test for Advanced License for Teaching, in addition to two tests for General License shall consist of: 1. Test of Knowledge of School Systems in USA, UK, China and India; 2. Test on ICT including developing of Computer Programs, and 3. Review of documents on Innovations and Action Researches and CAI undertaken during the year.

Administration of National Level and State Level Tests

The national level test shall be conducted in two languages: Hindi and English. NCTE may totally outsource the products and the process to some selected well-reputed agency. This may be done on contract basis, which may change at the instance of the NCTE. in no case the NCTE get involved in either stage except in the choice of the agency. For instance, NCTE may like to give this responsibility to an agency like Ed.-CIL to prepare Test Preparation Materials—Print and offer its E-version as well as CDs to accompany print version and also prepare actual tests. Regional Offices of NCTE may administer these tests with the help of SCERTs / IASEs of various States and issue appropriate Licenses. State authorities may give the task of developing State Specific tests by adapting in State language (other than Hindi), translation of the national level test or developing their own tests with the explicit permission of the relevant Regional Committee. The system should remain open to correction after a two-year mandatory evaluation.

For National level test, the higher secondary course to be covered by prospective elementary school teachers shall include the relevant examination material conducted by the Central Board of Secondary Education and the Council for Indian School Certificate Examination. Many States have already a mechanism in place for admission tests for various teacher education courses. They may utilize these agencies for the purpose of teacher recruitment tests as well.

SECTION - I

1

Teacher Education in the 21st Century: Promoting Health, Nutrition and Healthy Behaviours

S.P. Singh

Introduction

At the first decade of this new century and millennium, we are convinced that the future well-being of our nation and people depends not just on how well we educate our youth but also on how well we educate them about their health, nutrition and healthy behaviors. Each nation, no matter what its customs, wealth, or international status, has as one of its priorities the health of its youth. An American scientist, Benjamin Franklin aptly stated, "no nation can ever be stronger or healthier or more understanding than the strength, health, and understanding which is indicated in its youth." U.S. Surgeon General beautifully stated that "you can't educate a child who isn't healthy and you can't keep a child who is not educated." Health – a component of life is the foundation upon which the drama of life is enacted and without health all else is limited. According to James A. Brussels, M.D., an unbalanced diet has been shown to result in faulty learning and below-normal intelligence in children. George Watson in his book, "Nutrition and Your Mind" contends that mental and emotional disorders are almost entirely due to disturbance of body's metabolism which, he states, is the result of faulty diet. Another study cited by F. Monckebery, M.D. of Santiago, Chile, involving 400 pre-school children showed that poor nutrition may be largely to blame for delinquency.

The health problems that face adolescents in the United States are largely preventable and can be attributed to a few specific behaviors including poor nutrition, insufficient physical activity, substance abuse, early sexual activity and ever increasing chronic diseases (U.S. Department of Education). The obesity rate in children is rising alarmingly, Children and adolescents spend countless hours snaking on high-fat foods in front of the television set. Extended television watching and playing video/computer games contributes to physical inactivity—another factor contributing to obesity. A Primary Care Physician, Juhee L. Singh, M.D. 2007, recently stated that she has been seeing an increasing trend of eating disorders like anorexic nervosa, bulimia, and binge eating in adolescent population. Although the manifestations are physical, eating disorders have psychological roots, including low self-esteem, striving for control to offset the feeling of helplessness, depression and perfectionism. The elementary years are not too soon to head off tendencies toward eating disorders by promoting a healthy body image, encouraging exercise and activity, and providing factual information about the efforts of improper eating patterns (Weinstein and Rosen, 1999). Results from the 1999-2002 National Health and Nutrition Examination Survey (NHANES), using measured heights and weights, indicate that an estimated 16 percent of children and adolescents ages 6-19 years are overweight. This represents a 45 percent increase from the overweight estimates of 11 percent obtained from NHANES for 1988-1994 period. Epidemiological studies have identified several environmental factors including an increasingly sedentary lifestyle and the availability of energy-dense (high-fat, concentrated-sugar), low-fiber foods and increased consumption of sugar-added beverages and reduction of dairy intake have been associated with obesity in children and adolescents (American College of Physicians, 2006).

Recent statistics indicate that about one million children and adolescents in America are abused and neglected. Suicide and homicide are responsible for 35 percent of adolescent deaths. Four out of ten teenagers become pregnant before they reach the age of twenty and fifty percent of these drop out of school. Nearly one-quarter of adolescents have serious alcohols and drug use problems and this places them at greater risk of accidents. An Emergency Room Physician, Rahul P. Singh, M.D., 2007 stated that he had been seeing an increasing number of adolescents involved in auto accidents in recent years.

According to the National Commission on the role of the community in improving adolescent health, for the first time in our history, children are less healthy and less ready to take their place in society than their parents were. With the health status of children as our measure of health, U.S. society, especially the people in the education and teachers, have a commitment yet to be fulfilled. Although the United States spend more money on health care than any other nation in the world, however, health is a relatively low priority for our schools, as evidenced by the infrequency of health requirements in the K-12 curriculum. We do not apply the knowledge to a strong learning component about how students can influence their own health (Weinstein and Rosen, 1999). Unfortunately the classroom teachers, particularly those teaching K-12, who have the most excess to students but limited time, often are not prepared to include basic health education in their classrooms. This leaves teachers responsible to include health topics with little professional education or in-service preparations in health issues.

This paper is intended to encourage K-12 classroom teachers to take part in developing healthy behaviors in their students from the earliest point of these students education. Tomorrows teachers need to be more knowledgeable about, and more comfortable with health topics, more reflective in their practice of teaching about health, and better equipped with activities for incorporating health subjects into their existing curriculum. It may be added that unless the classroom teacher becomes more knowledgeable about health topics, health will not be seriously and permanently interesting to their students and the educators may not have significant influence on the health behaviour and lifelong choices of their students. As stated by Weinstein and Rosen that many things influence the commitment of K-12 classroom teachers to health education. Among them are their own personal interest in health, the personal responsibility they feel toward the health needs of their students, and the commitment of teacher-preparation programs to educate classroom teachers about health. The K-12 teachers need to acquire a working knowledge of the field of health and the delivery of health education. Most teachers have profound impact on students' health behaviors by the examples teachers set in eating habits, physical activities, substances use, and therefore, they are, unintentionally, health educators of a sort. The health behaviors their students observe in them consistently, and everyday, make teacher modeling especially influential. The classroom environment and health topics that can be integrated into the curriculum can have subtle but powerful effects on students. These efforts, not intended to compromise the traditional K-12 school curriculum, can make a difference in the ongoing health decision-making and prevention behaviors that students select to live healthier lifestyles.

Health and Health Education

The World Health Organization in 1947 defined health as "a state of complete physical, mental, and social well-being and merely the absence of disease or infirmity". Jonas Salk, who developed a vaccine for polio, believes health should be viewed not merely as freedom from disease but as actively growing, developing, and evolving. Hyman (1975) stated that the concept of health has several dimensions, each having its own continuum. The individual's ability to make decisions and interact socially, psychologically, and physically with society determines health. Dunn (1961) also reflected this viewpoint when he stated that optimal health or high-level wellness is an integrated method of functioning which is oriented toward maximizing the potential of which the individual is capable. It requires that the individual maintain a continuum of balance and purposeful direction within the environment where he or she is functioning.

The younger children begin the lifelong process of becoming healthy, the greater the possibility they will be successful. Teachers must recognize that children bring to schools many values and behaviors. These values represent both the beneficial and negative aspects of a child's living practices. According to Anspaugh and Ezell (1995), teachers should be aware of the powerful influences they exert in the lives of their students. No where in the entire educational spectrum can a teacher make such an impression as at the K-12 level. Consequently, the teacher who exemplifies a lifestyle conducive to high-level wellness, who exhibits a style of living that is physically, socially, and psychologically healthy, enhances the probability that his or her students will attempt to incorporate those beneficial aspects in their own lives.

Like health, the term health education can be defined in many ways, the Joint Committee on Health Education Terminology (1991) stated that the health education process is the "continuum of learning which enables people, as individual members of social structures, to voluntarily make decisions, modify, and change social conditions in ways which are health enhancing." Green and Kreutzer (1991) have defined health education as "any combination of learning experiences designed to facilitate voluntary actions conducive to health." According to Pollock and Hamburg (1984), health education is an applied science basic to general education of all children and adolescents. Its body of knowledge represents a synthesis of facts, principles, and concepts drawn from biological, behavioral, sociological and physical sciences but interpreted in terms of human needs, human values, and human potential. The ultimate goal of health education is the development of an adult whose lifestyle reflects actions that tend to promote his or her own health as well as that of family and community. From the K-12 teachers' perspective, health education is the process of developing and providing planned learning experiences in such a way as to supply information, change attitudes, and influence behavior. This process results in the child achieving individual responsibility for personal health, which leads to health enhancement, or high-level wellness. All this is accomplished through the teacher creating and facilitating learning experiences that develop the child's decision-making ability. With good decision making skills, the child will make better choices, about the personal, family, peer, and social factors, that influence the child's quality of life (Anspaugh and Ezell, 1995). The best argument for teaching health education is that health behaviors are the most important determinant of health status and there appears desperate need for effective health education due to the existing problems our society faces. Almost three out of five deaths among children and adolescents are due to motor vehicles. Fires and drowning account for 22 percent. Nutritional problems are related to over consumption and imbalances in the type's amount of food causing chronic and degenerative diseases later in life. In 1981, state child health agencies reported that more than one-quarter of a million school age children had vision and hearing problems. Children in single-parent families and in low-income families are likely to be in poor health and at risk of emotional problems. It would seem that the task of integrating health education is overwhelming. Health should be taught from kindergarten through twelfth grade, in a sequence that introduces concepts at appropriate learning levels. Health instruction should have stated goals, objectives, activities, and evaluation criteria. Health curriculum should include instruction in growth and development, mental and emotional health, personal and family lifestyles, nutrition, disease prevention and control, safety, drug use and abuse, and personal and community health. Teachers in K-12 classrooms should have training and competence to teach health concepts and relate these to the wellness of their students. Equally important for schools is to interact and work with the family and the community to maximize the potential for implementing healthy behaviours.

In this era of education reform in the 21st century, National Health Education Standards are critical to the healthy development of children and adolescents. National Health Education Standards improve student learning across the nation by providing a foundation for curriculum development, instruction and assessment of student performances. National Health Education Standards provide a guide for enhancing preparation and continuing education of teachers. The goal of the National Health Education Standards is improved educational achievements for students and improved health in the United States. Standards in health education help students achieve the educational goals set in America 2000: An Education Strategy and the Health Goals in Healthy People 2000: National Health Promotion and Disease Prevention. National Health Education Standards as published by American Association for Health Education are discussed below.

1. **Students will comprehend concepts related to health promotion and disease prevention to enhance health.**

The acquisition of basic health concepts and functional health knowledge provides a foundation for promoting health-enhancing behaviors among youth. This standard includes essential concepts that are based on established health behaviors theories and models. Concepts that focus on both health promotion and risk reduction are included in the performance indicators.

2. **Students will analyze the influence of family, peers, culture, media, technology and other factors on health behaviours.**

Health is impacted by a variety of positive and negative influences within society. This standard focuses on identifying and understanding the diverse internal and external factors that influence health practices and behaviors among youth including personal values, beliefs and perceived norms.

3. **Students will demonstrate the ability to access valid information and products and services to enhance health.**

Accessing valid information and health-promoting products and services is critical in the prevention early detection and treatment of health problems. This standard focuses on how to identify and access valid health resources and to reject unproven sources. Applying the skills of analysis, comparison and evaluation of health resources empowers students to achieve health literacy.

4. Students will demonstrate the ability to use interpersonal communication skills to enhance health and avoid or reduce health risks.

Effective communication enhances personal, family, and community health. This standard focuses on how responsible individuals use verbal and non-verbal skills to develop and maintain healthy personal relationships. The ability to organize and to convey information and feelings is the basis for strengthening interpersonal interactions and reducing or avoiding conflict.

5. Students will demonstrate the ability to use decision making skills to enhance health.

Decision-making skills are needed in order to identify, implement and sustain health-enhancing behaviours. This standard includes the essential steps needed to make healthy decisions as prescribed in the performance indicators. When applied to health issues, the decision making process enables individuals to collaborate with others to improve quality of life.

6. Students will demonstrate the ability to use goal-setting skills to enhance health.

Goal-setting skills are essential to help students identify, adopt and maintain healthy behaviors. This standard includes the critical steps needed to achieve both short-term and long-term health goals. These skills make it possible for individuals to have aspirations and plans for the future.

7. Students will demonstrate the ability to practice health-enhancing behaviours and avoid or reduce health risks.

Research confirms that practicing health enhancing behaviours can contribute to a positive quality of life. In addition, many diseases and injuries can be prevented by reducing harmful and risk taking behaviors. This standard promotes accepting personal responsibility for health and encourages the practice of healthy behaviours.

8. Students will demonstrate the ability to advocate for personal, family and community health.

Advocacy skills help students promote healthy norms and healthy behaviours. This standard helps students develop important skills to target their health enhancing messages and to encourage others to adopt healthy behaviours.

American Association of Health Education publishes several periodicals which include health support materials concerning health education promotion, responsibilities and competencies for teachers of young adolescents. These resources include lesson plans, ideas, activity sheets, coloring sheets, games, songs, poems and all materials are downloadable, printable and free. The American Journal of Health Education is the only journal of its kind to cover today's health education and health promotion issues head on with timely, substantive, and thought provoking articles for professionals working in medical care facilities, professional preparation, colleges and universities, community and public health agencies, schools and businesses. Features include news from the field, calendar events, buyers guide, new products and resources, and columns for community and school health educators.

International Electronic Journal of Health Education is the first peer reviewed electronic journal to serve the health education/health promotion field in the world. The journal creates global outreach and uses technology to reach health practitioners all over the world and is available to subscribers from around the globe.

Hextra is published four times a year and its circulation reaches health educators and covers events in all professional settings: schools, college/university, community/publish agency, medical care and business work place and covers the latest issues in health education.

HIV Prevention and CSHE Project Brief is a tri-annual publication of the American Association of Health Education. Each brief addresses a specific topic related to the goal of strengthening the professional preparation of elementary, middle school and special education teachers in health education, including HIV prevention education.

Nutrition and Healthy Behaviours

Proper nutrition means that all the essential nutrients—that is, carbohydrates, fats, protein, vitamins, minerals and water—are supplied and utilized in adequate balance to maintain optimal health and well-being. In 1979, the U.S. Surgeon General released a report advising Americans to "eat less saturated fats and cholesterol, less salt, less sugars and more complex carbohydrates such as whole grains, cereals, fruits, and vegetables, and relatively more fish, poultry, legumes, (such as peas, beans and peanuts) and less red meat". A well-balanced diet as published by Star and McMillan, 1995 constitutes daily portions of different foods groups. About 6-11 servings of carbohydrates including whole-grain bread, rice, pasta and cereal; about 2-5 servings of fruits and vegetables including apples, orange, mango and green leafy vegetables; about 2-3 servings of proteins including legume, nut, poultry, meat, milk, yogurt and cheese; and restricted intake of fats and simple sugars including butter, cream, candies and sweet desserts.

Helping students develop sound nutritional habits should be one of teachers' major goals in K-12 classroom health instruction. Increasing evidence supports the relationship between the immune system and eating behaviour. Poor eating habits and insufficient nutrients seem to play a significant role in lowering a person's ability to resist common viral and bacterial infections, and causing illness to be lengthier and more severe. A well- nourished student is more apt to reach his or her full potential physically, mentally and intellectually. Studies indicate that sound school nutrition programmes can produce positive results (Crockett, Mullis, and Perry 1988). The Healthy Schools Summit was held in Washington, D.C. in 2002, brought together the nation's leading education, children's health and nutrition organizations in a groundbreaking effort to help improve kid's health and educational performance through better nutrition and physical activity in schools. It was concluded at this summit that those schools that support good nutrition and physical activity as part of a total learning environment—produce healthy students. Healthy students are better able to develop and learn. Healthy students who achieve their education potential form healthy communities. Healthy communities build a healthy America. The crucial role that schools play in helping shape our children's future makes them an essential partner in promoting a healthy lifestyle. This is achieved by creating a healthy school environment by placing teachers in the classrooms who are committed and have working knowledge of health, nutrition and delivery of health education.

K-12 classroom teachers need to develop and foster in children a strong internal locus of control that allows children to feel that what they themselves do is a main force in their ability to be well and healthy. With this belief system children are more likely to choose behaviours that will positively influence their own health. They will seek medical opinion, ask lots of questions, and incorporate the information into their healthy choices.

Promotion of activity levels that will maximize health benefits associated with reduced disease risk and a better quality of life involves keeping students active throughout the day and reduce the amount of time spent in sedentary activities. Also, giving students the opportunity to develop movement skills and to develop an adequate level of fitness. In school, opportunities for increasing movement can be provided in the classroom, the lunchroom, the playground, and the gymnasium. Classroom teachers should be integrating movement into their teaching of academic disciplines regarding the relationship between an active lifestyle and the maintenance of health. Considering the immense problem with alcohol and drug abuse among adolescents, our teachers for the 21st century should be prepared with skills and knowledge necessary concerning the major drugs of abuse and their effect on the body as well as the biological, sociological, psychological and legal issues associated with drug use and abuse in our culture.

References

American College of Physicians. 2006. ACB Medicine. Vol. 1, Web M.D., 111 Professional Building, New York.

Anspaugh, David and Gene Ezell. 1995. Teaching Today' Health. Allyn and Bacon Publishing Company, 630 p.

Crockett, S., R. Mullis, and C. Perry. 1958. Parent Nutrition Education: A Conceptual Model. Journal of School Health. 58, (2); 53-57.

Dunn, H. L. 1961. High Level Wellness. Arlington, VA: Beatty.

Green, L.W. and M.W. Kreutzer. 1991. Health Education Planning: An Educational and Environmental Approach. Palo Alto: Mayfield.

Giorgianni, Salvatore J, 1998. Developing Strategies to Communicate About Health. The Pfizer Journal: 2, (1), 33-35.

Hoyman, H.S. 1975. Rethinking An Ecologic- System Model of Man's Health, Disease, Aging, Death. Journal of School Health. 45, (9)

Pollock, M. and M. Hamburg. 1984. Health Education: The Basic of Basics. Paper presented at Delbert Oberteuffer Centennial Symposium, April, 1984, Atlanta, Georgia.

Salk, J. 1978. What Do We Mean by Health? Health Education. January-February: 14-16.

Singh, Juhee L. 2007. Verbal Communication. Primary Care Physician. California.

Singh, Rahul P. 2007. Verbal Communication. Emergency Room Physician. Kansas.

Stare, Fredrick et al. 1980. Nutrition: A Scope Publication. The Upjohn Company. 112 p.

Starr, Cecile and Beverly McMillan. 1995. Human Biology. Wadsworth Publishing Company. 527p.

Weinstein, Estelle and Efrem Rosen. 1999. Teaching Children About Health. Morton Publishing Company. 612 p.

World Health Organization (WHO) 1946. Constitution of the World Health Organization, Geneva: World Health Organization.

2

Defining 'Guidance'

Andrew Tadie, Associate Professor of English
Department of English, Seattle University, USA

Four Classical Guides: Athena, Venus, Lady Philosophy, and Beatrice as Models for Teachers

Contemporary educational research often investigates the effectiveness of different modes of teaching upon groups of students having distinct natural learning styles. The purpose here is to explore what a literary analysis of four classical works of literature might reveal about improving effective teaching and learning today. First, a caveat: I do not intend to explain why these four works should be taught and continue to be taught to students following a classical curriculum, but rather to illustrate a few, ways four guides - or teachers - might still be useful to teachers today, that is, how four good guides, Athena in Homer's Odyssey, Venus in Virgil's Aeneid, Lady Philosophy in Boethius's Consolation of Philosophy, and Beatrice in Dante's Divine Comedy, can teach us something, about the art of being a good teacher. Essential to the plots of these four classical works is the central human character, who is guided by a wiser being. Athena and Venus are pagan divinities and Lady Philosophy and Beatrice are characters who have reached a level of wisdom and virtue beyond what ordinary human beings can possibly achieve.

These four good guides exhibit a number of characteristics that may be useful for teachers to consider. They know the right moments to intervene in and recede from the lives of those they guide, they know the ones they guide are susceptible to the guidance of others who are self-serving, and they know when they should allow a greater guide to replace them.

Our four stories also describe different reasons that motivate good teachers. Athena is motivated to guide only those younger students she recognizes as having great potential, especially those who lack the guidance of two parents, and she is only motivated to guide older students with personal qualities similar to her own. She knows she cannot help everyone, only a few. Venus loves to encourage and protect students from dangers they will encounter on their way to accomplishing great things, which she knows they themselves can hardly imagine they could ever achieve without her guidance. Dante's Virgil is the teacher who prepares students to be guided effectively by another guide, and then recedes, confident that what he has taught will be magnified by a greater teacher. Beatrice does likewise when she guides Dante to St. Bernard.

Lady Philosophy is a teacher who never forgets her best students after they have completed their studies, and she will come to their aid when they encounter great misfortune.

Athena intervenes less in wily Odysseus's life, because he is a master of the ways of contending in the world. She intrudes more frequently in Telemachus's life, mainly because, having grown to adolescence under his mother's tutelage, he has had no model in the prudent ways of kingly manhood. When Athena does intervene in the lives of Odysseus or Telemachus, it is usually by indirection, either by advocating on their behalf before Zeus or by appearing to these two men in disguise. Often her guidance is meant to negate the guidance of those who have influenced Odysseus and Telemachus in a negative way. For example, she assumes the form of Mentor when she advises Telemachus to leave the court in Ithaca where inhospitable suitors have taken charge and seek news of his father at the court of Nestor and of Menelaus.[1]

She knows them to be good rulers who will teach him important lessons of kingship, piety toward the gods, and the rites of hospitality.

Later, Athena appears as herself in Book XV to insist that Telemachus leave the comfortable life he is enjoying at Menelaus's court in Sparta and return to Ithaca. She sends him to Eumaios, the swine herder, who, she knows but does not reveal, is extending his hospitality to the disguised Odysseus seeking intelligence about affairs at court.[2]

In an earlier passage Athena revealed why she was motivated to be Odysseus's guide. Odysseus has returned to Ithaca without realizing he had finally reached home. He is alone except for the gifts he bears from Alkinoos, King of Phaiakia. When he comes upon a shepherd, Athena in disguise, who tells him that he is in Ithaca, Odysseus identifies himself as a Cretan trying to make his way to Pylos. Delighted that Odysseus has dissembled, Athena reveals herself saying, "You chameleon! Bottomless bag of tricks! ... Two of a kind, we are, contrivers, both.... I that am always with you in times of trial, a shield to you in battle, I who made the Phaiakians befriend you ... now I am here again to counsel you.... Patience, iron patience, you must show....

I cannot fail you in your evil fortune, coolheaded, quick, well-spoken as you are! No fear but I shall be there; you'll go forward under my arm when the crux comes at last. And I foresee your vast floor stained with blood, spattered with brains of this and that tall suitor who fed upon your cattle."[3]

In this exchange Athena explains her reason for choosing to be Odysseus's guide and protector; he is so much like herself: a wily warrior, a dissembler, a convincing inventor of fictions, and, above all, a model of practical wisdom.

Venus's motivation for guiding Aeneas is different from Athena's. She is, after all, his mother. Yet, her ways of guiding him are like those of Athena's: she advocates on his behalf with Jupiter and other divinities, just as Athena had done for Odysseus; sometimes she dissembles and at other times reveals her true self to Aeneas, just as Athena had done to Odysseus and Telemachus; she uses her own particular talents to influence others to aid the one she guides; and she maneuvers affairs such that he can be guided successfully by others.

Venus, in her own way, is as effective and versatile a rhetorician as Athena. She negotiates successfully with Jupiter, her superior, who assures her that Aeneas is fated to rule Lavinium, and his progeny shall rule for generations, when Rome shall rule the world.[4] She negotiates in a different mode with Cupid, her son, to cause Queen Dido to fall completely and compulsively in love with Aeneas,[5] and when Aeneas, ever pious in obedience to the gods, is ordered to leave the peaceable city of Carthage and make his way to Italy, she negotiates with Neptune in another mode to ensure that Aeneas will sail there safely.[6]

In addition to using her rhetorical skills of negotiation, she uses her particular gifts as the goddess of love to entice her husband Vulcan to craft splendid armor which she would give undisguised to her son, as he prepared for battle against Turnus and his allies: "When Venus's heart was troubled by Laurentine threats of war, she spoke to Vulcan breathing on her husband words of godly love: 'Dear my lord, I'd never put you to vain trouble or useless toil, for all the debt I owed the sons of Priam, and all my tears for Aeneas's cruel mischance. Now by Jove's order, he stands on Rutulan soil; this time I come to beg your sacred power of arms mother for son. They whet the steel for me - for those I love!' With that, her snow-white arms went round his neck - gently, warmly. He tensed, then felt a burst familiar of flame.... His wife smiled at the ruse; she knew her charms."[7] Venus does not dissemble here; she is artful in getting what she wants from a willing husband.

She is, however, as capable in dissembling as Athena. When Aeneas soon after landing at the newly established city of Carthage comes upon a maiden huntress, she informs him that he has landed at a place where Dido rules as an extraordinarily capable queen. In departing from her son, Venus let shine a glow about her head and her perfume filled the air so that he would know that the shepherdess was his mother. He called out to her: "What? Heartless again you tricked your son with empty shows. Why was your hand not laid in mine? Why could we not speak truth?"[8] But she left without answering his questions. He supposes that his mother is indifferent to him, but she knows that a future king cannot become a "mamma's boy," excessively reliant on his divine mother. He must become alert enough to discover good guides for himself, one of which, Dido, he will meet shortly, but before he does so, he sees from a prospect the city of Carthage being built: "Aeneas was awed: so vast, where once was camp-ground! The wonder of gates, and avenues paved, and crowds! Working like mad, those Tyrians; some at walls, some toiled at forts, surveying, or hauling stone; some marked out home sites and drew boundary lines.

They had their laws, their courts, their councilmen. Here they were dredging a harbor; there they laid a theater's undercroft, and cut tall columns out of a quarried cliff to adorn the stage....

In mid town was a pleasant, shady park ... where Dido built a temple to Juno, a huge vault filled with wealth and holiness."[9]

From Queen Dido Aeneas is taught how to build from scratch a city capable of becoming the center of a great civilization. From Dido, Aeneas learns skills of city planning and management he will apply later in Latium, which centuries later would develop into a great civilization.

Aeneas himself, born in a great civilization, had never before witnessed city planning at its best.

But before he reaches Italy, he is guided by another, through the world of the dead. The Sibyl is a priestly guide, a seer who possesses wisdom from Apollo. She speaks truth, as revealed to her by him. From her Aeneas learns that even kings need divine guidance from prophets.[10]

Both Athena and Venus guide effectively because they know how to employ artfully their own particular talents and because they know the talents and disposition of those they guide.

Our third guide, Lady Philosophy, is a teacher quite unlike either Athena or Venus. She differs from them in her temperament, in her reason for guiding, and in her relationship to the one she guides. She is like a professor who, years after her star student had graduated and become a success, sees that he has forgotten what she had taught him.

Anicius Manlius Severinus Boethius, born into an illustrious Roman family, was given a superior classical education, married a noble and virtuous wife with whom he had several distinguished sons. Like Cicero and Seneca before him, Boethius was a scholar and a statesman.

He wrote several scholarly works that became textbooks for students pursuing a liberal arts education, and later he became consul and Master of the King's Offices under Theodoric, an Arian. When Boethius attempted to establish ecclesiastical unity between Rome and the Catholic Empire in the East, he was accused of treason and sentenced to death by torture. After his downfall, he wrote his most famous work, The Consolation of Philosophy.

The work opens in Boethius's prison cell where he is attempting to distract himself from his fate by reading poetry inspired by the lyric and dramatic Muses. Appearing mysteriously onto this scene arrives in splendor a stern, commanding school mistress, Lady Philosophy: "A woman of majestic countenance whose flashing eyes seemed wise beyond the ordinary wisdom of men.

Her color was bright, suggesting boundless vigor, and yet she seemed so old that she could not be thought of as belonging to our age. Her height seemed to vary: sometimes she seemed of ordinary human stature, then again her head seemed to touch the top of the heavens. And when she raised herself to her full height, she penetrated heaven itself, beyond the vision of human eyes. Her clothing was made of the most delicate threads, and by the most exquisite workmanship; it had - as she afterwards told me - been woven by her own hands into an everlasting fabric. Her clothes had been darkened in color somewhat by neglect and the passage of time, as happen to pictures exposed to smoke. At the lower edge of her robe was woven a Greek letter pi, at the top the letter theta, and between them were seen clearly marked stages, like stairs, ascending from the lowest level to the highest. This robe had been torn, however, by the hands of violent men, who had ripped away what they could. In her right hand, the woman held certain books; in her left hand, a scepter."[11]

The design and embroidery of Lady Philosophy's robe signify the great chain of being, the unified hierarchy of all rational human knowledge from the lowest levels of practical wisdom (pi) to the highest level of theoretical knowledge (theta). The "violent men" who tore pieces from her robe are those specialists who suppose their particular discipline is the key to understanding all knowledge.

"When she saw the Muses of poetry standing beside my bed and consoling me with their words, she was momentarily upset and glared at them with burning eyes. 'Who let these whores from the theater come to the bedside of this sick man?' she said. 'They cannot offer medicine for his sorrows; they will nourish him only with their sweet poison. They kill the fruitful harvest of reason with the sterile thorns of the passions; they do not liberate the minds of men from disease, but merely accustom them to it. I would find it easier to bear if your flattery had, as it usually does, seduced some ordinary dull-witted man; in that case, it would have been no concern of mine. But this man has been educated in the philosophical schools of the Eleatics [i.e., Stoics] and the Academy [i.e., Platonists]. Get out, you Sirens; your sweetness leads to death. Leave him to be cured and made strong by my Muses.' And so the defeated Muses, shamefaced and with downcast eyes, went sadly away."[12]

Throughout the remainder of the work, she gradually consoles Boethius by answering in turn each of his many questions about whether justice exists in a world where good men seem so often to suffer and evil men seem so often to thrive. To each of his questions she listens patiently and answers them firmly, self-confidently, and thoroughly, because she knows his questions are genuine since they arise from a man intelligent but sick at heart.

In an important way Lady Philosophy is unlike the two guides we have already seen. She guides Boethius to a state of mind, or rather of soul, beyond that achieved by Odysseus under Athena's guidance, Aeneas under Venus's guidance, and even Dante under Beatrice's guidance.

Neither Odysseus nor Aeneas is transformed in any essential way by their divine guides, but Boethius is. By the end of the work his mind is at peace because he has acquired a higher understanding about Divine Providence and His relationship with the world and the human beings in it.[13]

Our fourth and final guide, Beatrice, does effect a transformation in the one she guides, but she differs from the other three guides. Unlike them, Beatrice's teaching transcends matters of practical wisdom, worldly destiny, and wisdom acquired from philosophical inquiry. There is an other-worldliness to her guidance, a transcendence Dante recognized in her person, when she was alive on earth, a transcendence that moves him still, in the direction of her world, the world of the blessed.

Like Lady Philosophy, Beatrice never dissembles, though like Athena and Venus she relies on others to help guide Dante. She enlists Virgil to guide Dante through Hell and Purgatory so he can be fit for her to guide him through the spheres of

Paradise.[14] She chooses Virgil because he, like Dante, is a great poet. As a student, Dante's model was Virgil because of his power over evocative language and his vision of Hell where the condition of souls after death corresponds to the life they led on earth. Beatrice, being among the blessed in heaven, can show Dante aspects of life-after-death that Virgil, for all his genius, cannot know, so that Dante can, in turn, guide others who read his Divine Comedy.

Each of these stories describe four different motives of those who are guided, as well as of those who guide. Odysseus is like the student who seeks the favor of a good guide because he recognizes the practical advantages of doing so in pursuing his own goals. Aeneas, who loves his guide as a son loves his mother, resembles that type of student who desires to attach himself so closely to his guide that he would limit his own development in the process. Boethius is that superior student who becomes so accustomed to success at every turn that when a great unforeseen disaster strikes is inept at coping with misfortune; remediation can only occur when a guide comes to him. And Dante is like that able student captivated by the beauty created by great artists, as well as the beauty of a saintly soul; when he desires to emulate them, he finds that imitating them is not an easy task; such modeling requires strenuous self-discipline.

The guide in each story has her own particular motive for guiding. Athena guides the able Odysseus because she knows he is a man who does not know himself in a fundamental way. He supposes his wandering will end once he reaches home, returns to his wife and son, and reclaims rule over his kingdom. However, as the soul of the prophet Teresias had revealed to Odysseus, he will not die at home but at sea while exploring the limits of the world, and as Odysseus explains himself to Dante in Canto 26, "Not fondness for my son, nor reverence for my aged father, nor Penelope's claim to the joys of love could drive out of my mind the lust to experience the far-flung world."[15] Knowing that Odysseus will abdicate the throne, Athena is more attentive in guiding Telemachus. She guides him more frequently and more conscientiously because he has greater need of it and because he will succeed his father as king. Unlike Odysseus, Aeneas yearns for peace, for the end of the war, and for the end of his wandering following the destruction of his native city. Yet, when he achieved that rest at Carthage, where he had a wife compelled to love him, an adoring stepmother for his son, a safe haven for his wandering band of refugees, and a kingship over a city thriving and at peace, Aeneas, much against his wishes, is fated to leave, never to rest, fated to play his role in the advancement of civilization.[16]

For a very different reason, neither does Dante find rest. Only Boethius has been led to an understanding that causes his soul to be at peace. Initially, he misused his solitude - a forced rest, probably in prison awaiting his execution - by distracting himself reading lyric and dramatic poetry, much as students today might spend countless hours listening to popular music, watching DVD's of movies, playing computer games, or reading titillating fiction. Only after contemplating deeply his previous studies in philosophy does Boethius come to understand that the deepest possible levels of human suffering and human joy can be understood only with a proper knowledge of human vice and human virtue. Only with this understanding is he able to achieve a state of rest, a virtuous soul at peace.

If Boethius's purpose is to describe the therapeutic benefits of studying philosophy deeply in order to understand the human situation within the nature of things, Dante's is to describe the journey of the soul being guided upward through the hierarchical order of human longing. If Dante's soul is not at peace, it is because his experiences are not essentially contemplative; rather he encounters sometimes frightful and sometimes mysterious places and people as he travels through Hell, Purgatory, and the spheres of Paradise. At the beginning of the story he had intuited God's splendor and he sought it, but his desire to approach God directly, by his own powers, is blocked by his sins of fear, fraud, and carnal temptation. Forced to abandon a direct and easy approach to God, he must take the long and hard road. But his work does not end at the end of that road. Having glimpsed the dynamic and beauteous splendor of God, he then devotes himself to the work of writing a compelling story that will serve as a guide to his readers.

If at the end Dante, the narrator, does not achieve rest, his experience of the ineffably transcendent divine energy inspires him to write the most sublime of Italian poems.[17]

These four stories describe guides with different personalities and motives that may assist teachers today assess their own native talents and motives: an Athena, particularly attentive to younger students who, lacking guidance of two parents, need direction in pursuing a virtuous life, as well as to capable older students who, craving independence, need guidance in tempering their pride and pleasures and in defending what is their own; a Venus, aware of her essential nature which she uses to help students become more aware of their future and the great thing, they can hardly imagine they could ever achieve; a Lady Philosophy, adept at guiding students firmly yet patiently when prolonged distress overwhelms their rationality; a Virgil, cooperating with other guides for the greater good of those being taught; and a Beatrice, motivating admiring students, in order to enlarge their understanding of that transcendent reality which is the source of their admiration.

In spite of the differences in these four stories about a relationship between a guide and the guided, there are certain similarities about these relationships that merit the attention of teachers in the twenty-first century: in each story the relationship is personal - one good guide at a time for each of those guided; in each story those guided have already intuited that a good guide is superior to them in some important way; and in each story the good guide never intervenes unnecessarily in the life of the one guided. These good guides know themselves and act such that the ones they guide come to know themselves and their particular strengths better, and these good guides never permit the ones they guide to become excessively dependent upon them, aiming instead to emancipate them as persons better able to direct their own life in a more enlightened way, with greater intelligence, discipline, and courage.

Notes

1. Homer, The Odyssey, trans. Robert Fitzgerald, New York: Vintage Classics, 1990, 26-27, 45.
2. Homer, 267-68.
3. Homer, 239-243.
4. Vergil, The Aeneid, trans. Frank O. Copley, Indianapolis: The Bobbs-Merrill Company, 1975, 9-11.
5. Vergil, 22-23.
6. Vergil, 113-114.
7. Vergil, 177-178,
8. Vergil, 12-15.
9. Vergil, 15.
10. Vergil, 110-12. See also Aeneas dialogue with Helenus, 59-62.
11. Boethius, The Consolation of Philosophy, trans. Richard Green, New York: Macmillan Publishing Company, (1962)1988, 3-4.
12. Boethius, 4-5.
13. Boethius, 114.

14. Dante Alighieri, The Divine Comedy, trans. John Chardi, New York: W. W. Norton & Company, 1997, 368-370.
15. Dante, 136.
16. Vergil, 11. See also 184-187 and Dante, 136.
17. Dante, 599-601.

3

Creating Knowledge/Creating Justice: Classroom Possibilities

Don Hufford

Introduction

On March 27, 1968, in a meeting of the United Nations Commission on Human Rights, Eleanor Roosevelt asked - and answered - a question which still reverberates in the hearts and minds of those who find no pause in the battle against social, economic, political, racial, and cultural injustices. The question: "Where after all, do universal human rights begin?" And the answer: "In small places, close to home. Such are the places were man, woman, and child seek equal justice, equal opportunity, and equal dignity."

Reflection upon Mrs. Roosevelt's words results in a painful reminder that human rights, although universal in expressed principle, are not universally available. Ongoing events across the globe - in far-away places, and even in small places close to home - remind us that justice as expressed through the social/political meaning of human rights, human dignity, and equal opportunity is a concept that is too often not an accessible reality.

On a more personal note, Mrs. Roosevelt's words give me pause to consider my profession as a teacher-of-teachers. If universal human rights begin in the "small places close to home" then one place of important justice-beginnings is in the K-12 schools across America. It is in these public - sometimes private - spaces that hopes, dreams, and visions of the possible may be conceived. And, it is in the classrooms that ideas conceived may be birthed into realities; not just of knowledge acquired and created, but of justice affirmed, achieved, and searched for. It is in the schools that an internalized belief in equal justice, equal opportunity, and equal dignity may find a place to flower; and in the flowering give birth to seedlings that may find a place to grow in the larger society.

There are constant reminders that "education is our hope for the future; it is the best source and means for countering those dangerous trends of prejudice, violence, and exclusion that plague our society (Puett, 264)." The struggles for a just, caring society take place not only in the marketplace, in the seats of government, in union halls, in the courts, or on the various other social/political fields of battle where power meets powerlessness. There is ample reason to be profoundly concerned about what is happening in our elementary, middle, and secondary schools. These are the "small places close to home" where opportunities exist to "provide the knowledge and skills that individuals need to succeed and pursue collective purposes such as instilling democratic values, providing a mechanism for equal opportunity, and establishing a sense of national (and world) community (McDonnel, 15)."

Individual teachers almost universally express a motivation: "I want to make a difference." Many even understand the concept of, and strive to be, "transformative intellectuals (Giroux)." In fact, the "transformation" motivation is imbedded in the mission statements of many schools of education. The school where I find an academic home states that its basic mission is to prepares future teachers to "transform self, schools, and society." This mission flows easily from the parent university's mission to encourage students to form "a critical consciousness that hungers and thirsts for justice and peace." Turning such well-meaning words into real-life actuality requires challenging the powerfully entrenched social/political/educational "what is" and working toward a social justice impregnated "what should be." This is not an easy task in a consumer-inspired world where pre-packaged standards for teacher education programs in America's universities tend more-and-more to mirror the "teach to the test" expectations emanating from a "No Child Left Behind" ideology.[1]

Encouraging and challenging future teachers to plant seeds that blossom into a student's hunger and thirst for peace and justice requires more that meeting formulaic, standardized, accreditation standards. Preparing soon-to-be-teachers to assume the role - in metaphorical language – of pedagogical chefs following standardized recipes is perhaps necessary to meet accreditation demands. Such professional grooming may be required to help forge a beginning foray into the teaching field. It is, however, insufficient preparation for engaging teachers in the struggle to incorporate a justice-driven mission into a classroom setting. A teacher's personal role in transforming society begins with classroom struggles that expand beyond knowledge transmission and acquisition. It requires more than teaching subjects in a way that leads to achieving passing scores on competitive tests. A teacher's transformative role begins with efforts to understand the conceptual meaning of, practicing the precepts, and teaching the principles inherent in, *justice*. And it begins in the "small places, close to home" that define neighborhood classrooms. Make no mistake, it is a struggle.

In counterpoint - even in direct opposition - to this struggle, the predominant educational language - translated into practice - in the educational system today is one of quantifiable and technical competency influenced by corporate-world definitional standards of "excellence." The focus is on standardized, high-stakes tests. It is on state and national assessments, on bottom-line efficiency based on a "free-market" competitive ideology, and on teacher accountability as measured by student scores.

Where is the mission-driven, ethically-sustainable effort to provide students in the "small places close to home" with the motivation, the knowledge-inspired vision, and the personal courage to eventually work toward a more justice-oriented world society?

> Too many schools fail to confront the racial, class, and gender inequalities woven into our social fabric. . . Classrooms can be places of hope, where students and teachers gain glimpses of the kind of society we could live in, and where students learn the academic and critical skills to make it a reality (Bigelow, 4).

Infusion of such hope into the classrooms begins with the educator who models, teaches, inspires, and challenges. It is the premise of this paper that schools of education in America's universities should find places in the curriculum to plant seeds of justice in the minds, hearts, and spirits of future teachers. This is possible, even in the face of growing accreditation standards and of academic expectations that, while stimulating a "teach to the test" mania, do little to encourage "teaching toward justice." There is ample reason to believe that "teacher educators *can* find various ways of incorporating concepts, attitudes, and skills related to education for peace and justice into the content and process of the teacher education programs (Haipt, 161)."

Thoughts to Ponder

In considering the schools of America as places where ideas of "universal human rights begin," we may be reminded of the insight of social justice pioneer, Jane Addams, in which she reminds us of the wonderful and inexplicable instinct for justice which resides in the hearts of man. This instinct may be cultivated or neglected . . . and it is never so irresistible as when the heart is young (Addams, 68).

To fail to cultivate this instinct in our students is not just to miss an opportunity; it is to lose our moral compass as educators. The existentialist psychotherapist, Erich Fromm, has written similarly of a pattern of psychological development which "results in such specific tendencies as . . . the striving for justice (Fromm)." Lawrence Kohlberg, in his research on the stages of moral development has defined "the virtue of justice" as one concept which is critical to both moral growth and the process of education. It would be a positive movement if future teachers were educated to understand justice as a virtue, and to pedagogically cultivate the striving for justice in students. The emphasis in schools of education tends, however, to move in another direction in deference to political and cultural power structures that define "what knowledge is of most worth," and what teaching "dispositions" best fit an instrumentalist model.

Today's established model for the "successful" teacher is one crafted from a combined neoliberal/neoconservative educational ideology. This way of thinking drives those reform movements which demand "world-class standards" designed to prepare students - in former president Bill Clinton's words - "to compete and win in the world economy." The predominant educational language spoken today is one of quantifiable and technical competency influenced by corporate-world definitional standards of "excellence." The focus is on standardized tests, state and national performance assessments, bottom-line efficiency, and teacher accountability measured by student "scores" reflecting a "free market" competitive philosophy. Maxine Greene, representing a philosophical challenge to this educational status quo, reminds us to be cautiously aware that

> (t)he dominant watchwords remain "effectiveness," "proficiency," "efficiency," and an ill-defined, one-dimensional "excellence." Reforms or no, teachers are asked to teach to the end of "economic competitiveness" for the nation. They are expected to process the young (seen as "human resources") to perform acceptably on some level of an increasingly systematized world . . . The orientation has been to accommodation, to fitting into existing social and economic structures, to what is given, to what is inescapably *there* (Greene, 1988, 12).

In an educational world of socialization to the status quo, it is all too easy for teacher education programs to focus with unreflective zeal on the "dominant watchwords." In so doing there is academic acquiescence to a behavioristic/technocratic/consumerist definition of the purpose of public education; one that reflects a sociologically referenced structural-functionalism.[2] So defined, schools are organized in terms of an ideologically tinged No Child Left Behind, standards driven, teach-to-the-test, free market inspired processing of raw materials (students) into a pre-planed product (world-class workers). Students are oriented toward - and compared against - a testable "success model" that places primary value on socialization to an existing economic/social system, rather than on developing the motivation and abilities to critically question and transform the "inescapably there."

Fortunately, there are activists, albeit on the fringes of the educational power structure, who are inspired by counterpoint social/political philosophies. These modern day prophets - defined in part as those who "ask the challenging questions (Heschel)" - do not rest easy with the educational status quo. They ask the challenging questions, and seek answers in constructive communal dialogue about the purposes and methods of education. They understand that teaching "must be rooted in eliminating social injustices as well as creating pedagogical practices that help students to imagine a different and better world (Giroux, 290)," and they serve as "moral agents fulfilling a universal claim for justice (Veroli, 198)."

These educational radicals engage in prophetic dialogue, and stress that a focus on issues of equality, dignity and justice, should have a definitive place in the curricula of teacher education programs. Questions need to be raised about the broader issues of educational purpose; issues that expose the limitations of a system based on a test-driven, global economic competitiveness. The schools of America are "those places close to home" where questions about equal justice, equal opportunity, and equal dignity must not just be asked, but intellectually explored as economic, social, racial, cultural, and political issues. We are reminded that "education . . . can provide important tools needed to alleviate human suffering and promote justice (Jenness, 2)." Our teachers need to relate to this possibility; to understand that what happens in the individual classroom cannot be isolated or divorced from the broader, invasive, problematic societal concerns. Future teachers should be helped to use an understanding of the sociology of knowledge in critically examining the ideological underpinning of the educational process. Teachers "have to understand the importance of being part of a larger struggle. It is not enough to teach well and create a social justice classroom separate from the larger community (Kohl, 1998, 286)." Here - in the classroom - is an opportunity for critical inquiry and dialogue to be engaged in, and reflected upon. The teachers-to-be who will soon be in America's classrooms need to be helped to understand that the opportunity is also a responsibility.

It is not enough for teacher education programs to provide the technical and methodological skills defined in the literature as "best practices." It is not enough for the teacher educators' partners in the "arts and sciences" to provide a knowledge base in the various academic disciplines to be taught at the secondary school level. The technical skills and content knowledge that are so important to the *becoming* teacher are "necessary but not sufficient" preparations for the task of teaching in America's schools. Teaching - particularly in the public schools - should be defined as a "democratic" task. It is a task relating to interpreting and understanding the social/political structure of a democratic, pluralistic, ever-changing society. It is not a task for the faint hearted.

> Democratic educators seek not simply to lessen the harshness of social inequalities in school, but to change the conditions that create them . . . (They) care deeply about young people, but they also understand that such caring requires them to stand firm against racism, injustice, centralized power, poverty, and other gross inequities in school and society (Beane and Apple, 12).

It a premise presented here is that schools of education should accept a challenge to transfuse the profession with "democratic educators." Such educators understand that to "care deeply" is to stand firm against injustice; it is to challenge and to question an ideological power structure; it is to "teach against the grain (Simon);" it is to become "transformative intellectuals who will be leaders affecting substantial educational change (Hayes, 67)." As Roger Soder has reminded us, "... fundamental notions (dispositions toward justice) must be part of the repertoire of all teachers, part of their working knowledge (Soder, 261)." This repertoire, this set of possibilities, this epistemological framework, will provide the teacher with motivation to transgress the boundaries of traditional educational practice.

> The classroom remains the most radical space in the academy . . . urging us to open our minds and hearts . . . to make education the practice of freedom . . . (T)he classroom, with all its limitations, remains a location of possibility. In that field of possibility we have the opportunity to labor for freedom, to demand of ourselves and our comrades, an openness of mind and heart that allows us to face reality even as we collectively imagine ways to move beyond boundaries, to transgress. This is the practice of freedom (hooks, 12 and 207).

The K-12 classroom - that small place close to home - remains a "location of possibility" where a societal future is being built. The classroom - particularly the public school in urban areas - is a microcosm of the social/political macrocosm. Diverse social, political, and epistemological issues related to individual worldviews - and the psychological/sociological dynamics of particular group memberships (racial, cultural, gender, religious, economic) - are classroom realities. "Different social standpoints yield different views of the world . . . This is the classic proposition in the sociology of knowledge (Connell, 123)." Here is where - as Mrs. Roosevelt reminds us - the "wonderful and inexplicable instinct for justice . . . may be cultivated or neglected." Here is where "solutions to racism, sexism, classism, and other forms of prejudice, are lived and taught in small daily increments (Rehak, 240)."

But solutions are only to be found where questions are raised, problems made known, and the practice of freedom engaged in. Boundaries must be transgressed, educational orthodoxies challenged, and educational priorities redefined. It is possible to "re-imagine education, to think clearly about justice and possibility (Clinton)." For the educator, this kind of thinking implies an activist involvement in expressing the meaning and implications of justice and injustice within the educational system, and within the wider social/political community.

A transformed society may well begin in small, daily increments in small places close to home, the schools; places where students are taught to think about the meaning and the methods of justice. This will happen only if those who teach in the classrooms across America are motivated, willing, and able to be catalysts for change, and not just skilled pedagogues and dispensers of testable knowledge. Here is a role for schools of education. If teachers-of-teachers are to influence the direction of societal transformation then they must think clearly about justice and possibility. They must encourage their students to ask probing questions about what should be expected from our teachers, our schools, and from the social/political/economic system we call "education."

Taking Risks, Encouraging Dissent, Educating "Radicals"

Education in the United States today is infused (I might say infested) with the same ideologically-driven goals that are so powerfully evident in the broader social, economic, cultural, and political spheres. The politically inspired, and misnamed, *No Child Left Behind Act,* gives an additional voice to an educational orthodoxy that is powered by the force of a pervasive political agenda. Teachers are disempowered, curricula are standardized, procedures are regimented, creativity is bureaucratically stifled, and - in obeisance to a market mentality - students are redefined as products and parents as consumers. A "teach-to-the-test" mantra sounds throughout the land. John

Dewey's concept of democratic education finds "no room at the inn;" except where there are risk-takers willing to challenge the prevailing educational status quo.

It is a thesis of this paper that the nation's schools of education have choices. They can surrender to *what is*, or use the power of teacher education to encourage future educators to "re-imagine" what *should be* in terms of a society - even a world - of equal justice, equal opportunity, and equal dignity for all. Teachers should be educated to be more than highly trained, licensed technicians; more than standardized conformists to a pattern developed and enforced by a power structure that controls the professional accrediting process. Teachers should be educated to understand, to accept, and to fulfill the responsibility to challenge all that interferes with a just and open social system.

Teaching can be more than knowledge transmission, or even knowledge creation; it can be a force for a continually-emerging just and caring society. "If we can learn to think critically and creatively, we can learn to think caringly (Lipman, 115)." Teachers should be educated to be critical intellectuals who have the courage, the moral authority, and the professional opportunity to think caringly; to challenge injustices and inequities wherever they exist. Future teachers should be educated to use the classroom not only to dispense officially sanctioned knowledge and testable facts, and to conform to standardized, pre-established expectations; but also to engage in the transformation of society.

Wow!! What a responsibility for a teacher. Here is an expectation that rises above opening doors to the world of the 3-Rs, job-related skills, academic content, and to the "adventures" of high-stakes testing. Here is a responsibility to be passionate advocates for a just society, a better world, and a hopeful future for all. Here is a recognition that teaching "requires passion, a humanist vision and a critical posture. It can stir the soul, expand the imagination, impart critical skills, energize the body; and secure justice, compassion, empathy, and ecological sustainability (Kincheloe, 1)." Preparing future teachers for this responsibility presupposes exposing them to complex questions; questions regarding *why* and *how* do teachers, schools, and society need to be transformed; and *who* and *what* are impediments to the transformative process. And, of course, it involves preparing future teachers for what are often disconcerting and difficult to accept answers. It requires listening to the voices of diverse others. It requires open-ended dialogue, and open-mindedness. It requires risk-taking. To encourage this "disposition" in those who would be teachers, we who are teacher educators need to

> nourish a social imagination, the capacity to look at the world as it could be otherwise, as well as a spirit of activism combined with skepticism, urgency, and patience. We act, we doubt. The time is late and we have a long way to go (Ayers, 158).

This teaching, a "teaching toward justice," is not a job for conformists, but for radicals. Educational conformists follow the path of least resistance, a path created and mapped by someone in power. Radicals are more curious, prone to challenge the power structure, to ask hard questions, and to embrace the intellectual challenge created by paradoxical, conflicting answers. "It is radical to wonder *why* (Breton, 437)," but asking the *why* of educational policy, procedures, purposes, and methods should be part of every teacher's academic/professional preparation. And, of course, powerful *why* questions lead inexorably to how, what, and who questions. And, these questions cover a broad range of educationally-related issues. A teacher's education has been stunted if he/she has not been pushed to ask questions seemingly - but, in reality, not - extraneous to educational content and method. Educational questions are often related to,

> inequalities between the haves and the have nots . . . race, ethnicity, class, nationality, gender, sexual orientation, (dis)ability, religion . . . erosion of civil rights . . . immigration . . . the privatization of public services . . . . . . environmental degradation . . . global warming . . . and other social problems (Jenness, 1).

Such problematic social issues impact teachers at every level, and it is important to understand that these issues

> (a)re linked to societal systems of power . . . At the heart of practice, we must understand that every educator is a social activist . . . We cannot be released nor escape from our responsibility for affecting the wider world in which we live . . . In order to realize possibilities for a more just world, we need to recognize how power operates even through the most mundane educational activities (Wilson and Cervro, 4-5).

Every teacher education program should provide at least one academic venue for future teachers to explore activist dispositions; where questions about the agendas and motivations of established authority provide fuel for spirited dialogue. Too often, however, a teacher education program is designed primarily to prepare teachers to socialize students into the existing social/economic/political system. There is, in such a socializing program, an echo of Emile Durkheim's belief that the function of an educational system "is to adapt the child to the social milieu . . . It is, then, up to the State to remind the teacher constantly of the ideas, the sentiments that must be impressed upon a child to adjust him to the milieu in which he must live (Durkheim, 79)."

Democracy and social justice may be better served when, rather than adjustment to the established social milieu, we encourage and facilitate in the teacher education student a "creative maladjustment." To creatively maladjust is to dare to question and challenge the current social/political/educational system, rather than engage in unthoughtful, unreflective, lock-step marching to an ideological cadence. It is to find wisdom in Emerson's dictum that "a foolish consistency is the hobgoblin of small minds." Herbert Kohl has written of the "ability to break patterns (144)," and he reminds us that "teaching well is a militant activity . . . It requires developing the courage to maladjust rather than adjust oneself to much of current educational practice (144-45)." To question and challenge the system - to maladjust - may be a radical departure from standard teacher education protocol. It may, in reality, be a challenge to the very power that sanctions and accredits the model within which teachers function. But the questions must be asked, the challenges must be expressed.[3]

The teacher, at every level, does have a responsibility to respond to how power as a political, social, and/or economic force impacts education. Can a teacher be anything but a discontented dissenter when he/she evaluates the realities of unequal, and often unjust power structures and relationships in society? Ninety years ago in *Crisis* magazine, W.E.B. Du Bois issued a challenge to teachers that still reverberates down the halls of America's schools; we have only to listen . . . and respond.

> To be silent when injustices call out for redress, to fail to speak out when poverty and ignorance keep some in social bondage, to muffle the sounds of indignation and righteous anger, is to fail the teachers calling (Du Bois in Huggins, 157).

Indignation and righteous anger are appropriate responses to powerful neoliberal (and neoconservative) voices that speak for vested-interest groups whose market-driven goal is "the installation of *competition* in education at every level (between students, between teachers, between types of schools, between school districts) as the central organizing principle of human relationships (Marginson, 209)." Here we hear talk of for-profit privatization of the schools, outsourcing of various functions (i.e. food, custodial, security, and transportation services), vouchers, competitive "one-size-fits-all" accountability, etc. In challenging this corporate-styled organizing principle we are reminded that "a dissenting voice is sometimes needed to moderate the din made by enthusiastic multitudes (Postman, 1993, 5)." And . . . the most powerful multitudes are those that have economic, political, religious, or cultural agendas to promote; agendas that are not congruent with Eleanor Roosevelt's call for equal justice, equal opportunity, and equal dignity.

Another multitude, though one more passive than passionate or powerful, is composed of those K-12 teachers who uncritically accept social, political, and educational orthodoxies; those who are ill-prepared to challenge entrenched power structures; those who do <u>not</u> translate the power of knowledge into dissenting challenges to social injustices; those who are transformed by the system, rather than being transforming catalysts for a more just society. Perhaps part of the problem lies with the schools of education who prepare future teachers to "teach to the test," rather than to open their minds to larger possibilities. That is why "debating how teacher education should be carried on and judged is one of the most important things about which we can and must argue (Apple, xii)."

I am reminded that historically the original institutions for teacher preparation were called normal schools. The somewhat disconcerting fact is that the word "normal" is derived from the Latin, meaning "to conform to a rule or pattern." Does today's average school of education in the American university still function as a normal school; training future teachers to conform to patterns? As we consider the answer - or, perhaps paradoxical answers - to this question, we will intellectually wrestle with the proposition that our schools of education should not submit meekly to conformist expectations based on cookie-cutter standards and "outcomes." We might want to consider the thought that "the purpose of education is to create a mind which is explosive, and does not conform to a pattern which society has set (Krishnamurti, 26)."

It is the explosive mind that is motivated to "think outside of the box;" to think about the larger social picture; to ask questions about social justice issues; to challenge systems that deny "equal justice, equal opportunity, equal dignity;" to question and challenge the power of unilaterally imposed, and politically motivated, rules and patterns. It is the explosive mind that keeps democracy alive. And where is the fuse first lit? In those small places close to home – the classroom.

The Social Foundations Classroom

W.E.B. Du Bois once wrote of teaching as "a sacred trust for the education of a new and redeeming generation of men," and added: "This may be a dream but it is worth considering (quoted in Provenzo, 285)." Here was a radical proposal – to consider education as a means of redemption; not as a religious phenomenon, but nevertheless as a regenerating process of individual and social transformation. The idea may be so radical in an era of measurable accountability and standardized conformity that it can only begin as a dream. But, it is a dream which can be the foundation stone of an emerging reality.

One place to stimulate radical dreaming in America's teachers - including dreams of a just social system - is a social foundations of education classroom.[4] Here is perhaps the only place within the typical teacher education program where a questioning exploration of teaching as a subversive activity (Postman and Weingartner) is not only a pedagogical option, but an intellectual and moral necessity. For the teacher, to be a subversive is to be a "transformative intellectual." It is to be, in the words of Abraham Heschel, a prophet, one who "feels fiercely . . . who asks the challenging questions (5)." Too often a teacher education program is permeated with formulaic answers designed to satisfy an accreditation process and the testing phenomenon, rather than with critical analysis and thoughtful questions. Too often predetermined answers saturate the curriculum, and negate the intellectual problematic of significant, unasked questions.

> The gridlock of the testing movement is testing all of us. Powerful responses should be forthcoming from foundation scholars. If we manage to draw in our students, engage them in critical conversation, then move them beyond it, to action, we are fulfilling our role. To doanything else is to fall short, to be guilty of . . . not teaching our students (Meyer and Storz, 66).

While preparing future teachers for the world of educational reality, we should also charge them with the responsibility to ask the challenging questions about the *why* and the *who* of that reality. *Why* does the reality of disempowered teachers exist, and *who* has defined the parameters of what a teacher should know and be able to do? What vested interests have been at work in establishing standards, defining the "highly qualified teacher," and creating and profiting from high-stakes testing materials? And there is that important question which expands the boundary of a teacher's responsibility: in what ways can a teacher in "small places close to home" affirm universal rights and work toward a world of equal justice, equal opportunity, and equal dignity for all?

It is in the social foundations classroom that a future teacher may be challenged to experiment with the prophet's role, and to understand that "prophets (are) shocked not only by acts of injustice on the part of scoundrels, but also by the perversion of justice on the part of the notables (Heschel, 202)." Notables - those sitting in the seats of educational, political, and economic power - are not immune from inserting hidden agendas into educational policies and procedures; agendas that often serve to restrict opportunities for an equal and just society.

If a teacher is to "make a difference," it is important to be prepared to analyze and interpret- and critically question - these agendas; particularly those that are "linguistically airbrushed" to disguise hidden meanings. It is important that teachers have been prepared to give attention to the broader social, political, historical, and cultural forces that impact the schools of America.[5] Making a difference, of course, will most often be accomplished in small steps.

> In the final analysis what's important is not that classroom teachers assume the impossible burden of individual responsibility for solving all the social and educational problems . . . What matters is that they see the connections between these classrooms and the society around them, and realize that efforts to apply critical teaching are tied to broader efforts to promote democracy and equality in society (Karp, 166).

Perhaps, as educators, we will always stand on the threshold of possibility, wrestling with the door that opens into visions of a totally just society. But, in the wrestling we grow intellectually and emotionally stronger; more capable of translating hopes and dreams into reality. It may be that teachers in "those small places close to home"

> will be able to help future generations of thinkers and doers recognize the wisdom in the words of Mother Theresa: "We do no great things, only lots of small things with great love." As teachers-of-teachers "we must be willing, then, to act for small changes rather than waiting for some monumental movement when everything will fall into place (Ayers, 119)." In the social foundations classroom, as we seek to model a "teach toward justice" pedagogy, we may hear echoes of "the teaching of Rabbi Tarfon, who asserted that 'it is not your duty to complete the work, but neither are you excused from participating in it' (Shapiro, 204)."[6]

Concluding Reflection

The thoughts noted above are not validated by empirical research, as will be the ideas presented in so many papers presented at this conference. They do, however, connect existentially and epistemologically to an expressed concern germane to the conference: "the desire of many colleagues and students who sincerely want to 'make a difference' by contributing to the amelioration of social problems . . . in a way that leaves us a more just community at the local, state, national, and international levels (Jenness, 1-2)." The struggles for more just communities are carried out in many social arenas, including "those small places close to home" where America's teachers have an opportunity <u>and</u> a responsibility to open minds to real-world realities, and to possibilities to improve on the realities. We can empower young people to think beyond the emphasis on test-taking efficiency as a primary educational goal, and to reflect upon how they can be part of creating a community and world society of justice and equality.

My students, preparing to be teachers in America's K-12 schools, almost universally say they have chosen teaching because they "want to make a difference." The question must be raised: what does "to make a difference" mean? Is the meaning of the phrase limited to change in individual lives; to helping students become more successful, creative, happier, productive, self-affirming — to be socialized toward personal achievement within the status quo? Individual change is, of course, important. But, there is a larger, more in-depth interpretation of "making a difference" as a teacher. It is to visualize "teaching toward social justice." It is to "teach so that the young may be awakened to the joy of working for transformation . . . so that they may become healers and change their worlds (Greene, 1998, xiv)."

We who profess to be teacher educators in America's universities should recognize that to transmit, or even create, knowledge and skilled expertise is not adequate. We are reminded that "knowledge of what is does not open the door to what *should be* (Einstein, 42)." What *should be* is a more just and equitable society. The classroom can be a place of small-beginnings where visions of healing and transformation may be given birth. If this is to happen then teachers-to-be must be *educated* to be midwives of transformative possibility, and not just *trained* as knowledgeable and skilled pedagogical technicians capable of efficient transmission of preordained, officially sanctioned "worthwhile" information.

Notes

1. Social foundations scholars have recognized that in teacher education programs, the alignment of curricula with content information found in certification tests clearly threatens to undermine the role of Social Foundations courses as these tests and the curricula that support them

fail to measure the sorts of "counter- cultural sensibility" needed by teachers to resist or respond to the economic and political contexts impacting schoolsand communities (Martusewicz, 101).

2. In reference to schools, sociologists recognize two significant understandings woven into structural-functionalism theory: (1) There are certain universals, "values" that are necessary for the stability of a given society, and (2) schools represent the institutional setting for transmitting these values, and for socializing the young into the society's dominant social/political/economic system. In counterpoint to this sociological theory is the transformational-conflict approach that assigns schools a questioning, challenging, transformative role in regard to the status quo.

3. W.E.B. Du Bois, one of America's first research sociologists (see *The Philadelphia Negro)*, understood the importance of the critically penetrating question: "There are questions so fundamental that not to ask them is to die (1976, 334)"

4. It is to be noted that the Committee for Standards and Accreditation for the Council for Social Foundations of Education has stated (2002) in Principal #5 that the educator should be able to "specify how issues such as justice, social inequality, concentrations of power, class differences, race and ethnic relations, or family and community organizations affect teaching and schools."

5. It is in the social foundations classroom that these broader, powerful forces - and their influence upon education - are explored and critically interrogated. "There is a powerful tradition that characterizes the social foundations of education as an integrated multidisciplinary approach to

the study of education that focuses on the triadic relationship among social conditions, values, and educational policies (Washburn, 72)."

6. There is a similar social justice axiom, pregnant with interpretive possibility, woven into the words of the existentialist Jewish theologian, Abraham Heschel: "Not all are guilty, but all are responsible (16)."

References

Addams, Jane. Quoted in *Progressive*, January, 1999, 68.

Apple, Michael. 2005. "Introduction," *Trivializing Teacher Education: The Accreditation Squeeze*, eds. Dale Johnson, Bonnie Johnson, Stephen Farenga, and Daniel Ness. New York: Rowman & Littlefield Publishers, Inc.

Ayers, William 2002. *Teaching Toward Freedom.* Boston: Beacon Press.

Beane, James, and Michael Giroux. 1995. *Democratic Schools.* Alexandria, Virginia: Association for Supervision and Curriculum Development.

Bigelow, Bill. 1994. "Introduction," *Rethinking Our Classrooms: Teaching for Equity And Social Justice.* Milwaukee: Rethinking Schools.

Clinton, Hillary. 1999. "Re-Imagining Education: A Matter of Justice and Possibility." Lecture at Teachers College, Columbia University. April

Connell, R.W. 1993. *Schools and Social Justice.* Philadelphia: Temple University Press.

Du Bois, W.E.B. 1976. *Worlds of Color.* Millwood, New York. Kraus-Thomson Organization.

______. 1986. *W.E.B. Du Bois: Writing,* ed.. Nathan Huggins. New York: The Library of America.

Durkheim, Emile. 1956. *Education and Sociology,* trans., Sherwood Fox. New York: The Free Press.

Einstein, Albert. 1962. *Ideas and Opinions.* Trans., S. Bargmann. New York: Crown Publishers, Inc.

Fromm, Erich. 1961. *Escape from Freedom*, twenty-second printing . New York: Holt, Rinehart, and Winston.

Giroux, Henry. 1988. *Teachers as Intellectuals: Toward a Pedagogy of Learning.* New York: Bergin and Garvey.

______, 1998. "An Activist Forum V," *Teaching for Social Justice,* eds. William Ayers, Jean Ann Hunt, and Therese Quinn. New York: Teachers College Press.

Greene, Maxine. 1988. *The Dialectic of Freedom.* New York: Teachers College Press.

______, 1998. "Introduction," *Teaching for Social Justice*, eds. William Aayers, Jean Ann Hunt, and Therese Quinn. New York: Teachers College Press.

Hayes, Michael., Donna Grace, and Neil Pateman. 1998. "Reconfiguring the Preservice Curriculum," *Inquiry: Critical Thinking Across the Curriculum.* Spring

Heschel, Abraham. 2000. *The Prophets*, 3rd printing. Peabody, Massachusetts: Prince Press.

Haipt, Mildred. 1986. "Education," *Justice and Peace Education: Models for College and University Faculty,* ed. David Johnson. Maryknoll, New York: Orbis Books.

hooks, bell. 1994. *Teaching to Transgress: Education as the Practice of Freedom.* New York: Routledge.

Jenness, Valerie. 2007. *Call for Papers and Program Participation.* Society for the Study of Social Problems. http:// sssp1.org/ index.cfm/m/267. December.

Karp, Stan. 1994. "Why We Need to Go Beyond the Classroom," *Rethinking Our Classrooms: Teaching for Equity and Social Justice.* Milwaukee: Rethinking Schools.

Kincheloe, Joe., P. Slattery, and S. Steinberg. 2000. *Contextualizing Teaching.* NewYork: York: Longman

Kohl, Herbert. 1994. *I Won't Learn from You: And Other Thoughts on Creative Maladjustment.* New York: The Free Press.

---______, 1998. "Some Reflections on Social Justice," *Teaching for Social Justice*, eds. William Ayers, Jean Ann Hunt, and Therese Quinn. New York: Teachers College Press.

Krishnamurti, Jiddu. 1974. *On Education.* New York: Harper and Row,

Lipman, Matthew. 1996. *Natasha: Vygotskian Dialogues.* New York: Teachers College Press.

Marginson, Simon. 2006. "Engaging Democratic Education in the Neoliberal Age," *Educational Theory*, Vol. 56, No. 2.

Martusewicz, Rebecca. 2006. "Editor's Corner." *Educational Studies.* April.

McDonnell, Lorraine. 2000. "Defining Democratic Purposes," *Rediscovering the Democratic Purposes of Education,* eds., Lorraine McDonnell, P.M. Timpane, and Roger Benjamin. Lawrence: University Press of Kansas.

Meyer, Andy, Sabik and Mark Storz. 2004. "Laying the Foundations for Educational Foundations. *Educational Foundations.* Winter.

Postman, Neil. 1993. *Technopoly: The Surrender of Culture to Technology.* New York: W.W. Norton & Company.

Postman, Neil and Charles Weingartner. 1969. *Teaching as a Subversive Activity.* New York: Dell Publishing Company.

Provenzo, Jr., Eugene. 2002. *Du Bois on education.* New York: AltaMira Press.

Puett, Tiffany. 2005. "On Transforming Our World," *CrossCurrents.* Summer.

Rahak, Jay. 1998. "An Activist Forum IV," *Teaching for Social Justice*, eds. William Ayers, Jean Hunt, and Therese Quinn. New York: Teachers College Press.

Simon, Roger. 1992. *Teaching Against the Grain: Texts for a Pedagogy of Possibility.* New York: Bergin and Garvey.

Shapiro, H. Svi. 2006. *Losing Heart: The Moral and Spiritual Miseducation of America's Children.* Mahwah, New Jersey: Lawrence Erlbaum Associates.

Soder, Roger. 1996. "Teaching the Teachers of the People," *Democracy, Education, and the Schools,* ed., Roger Soder. San Francisco: Jossey-Bass Publishers.

Veroli, Nic. 2006. "Communism After Marx," *Radical Philosophy Review.* Vol. 9, No. 6.

Washburn, David. 1993. "Reinventing the Social Foundations of Education," *Educational Foundations.* Fall. .

Wilson, Arthur, and Ronald Cervero. 2001. "Adult Education and the Struggle for Knowledge and Power: Practical Action in a Critical Tradition." A presentation for the Adult Education Research Conference, Michigan State University.

SECTION - II

4

Teacher Education in India – then and now

(Education Commission (1964-66) –revisited)

R.P. Singh

"Teachers are prepared in hurry, rather than matured." Lord McNair

"I pretend to work here -they pretend to pay me." Internet Humor

(The International Context: According to the history as traced in the Britannica, (2001) "The earliest formal arrangements for teacher preparation, introduced in some of the German states during the early part of the 18th century, included both pre-service and in-service training. A seminary or normal school for "young men who had already passed through an elementary, or even a superior school, and who were preparing to be teachers, by making additional attainments, and acquiring a knowledge of the human mind, and the principles of education as a science, and of its methods as an art" was set up in Halle in 1706. By the end of the century there were 30 such institutions in operation in Germany. Systematic training was linked to an equally systematic process of certification, control of teaching conditions, and in-service study. All public teachers were required to attend a series of meetings to extend their practical knowledge."

The subsequent history of teacher training has linkages with what was started in Germany. Nineteenth-century developments in education in the United States, Britain, France, Belgium, and Japan owed much to the pattern that had been established in Germany. In France at the time of the French Revolution efforts were made to set up a system of normal schools. The École Normale (later the École Normale Supérieure), founded in 1794, closed after a few months; but it was reestablished by Napoleon in 1808 to train teachers for the lycées. After 1833 a uniform system of Écoles Normales (initially only for male students) was created, and the normal-school systems of several countries date from the third decade of the century. During the first 30 years of the 19th century, teacher preparation in the United States, Britain, and elsewhere was dominated by the monitorial methods introduced by Andrew Bell and Joseph Lancaster. In the simplest terms, the method involved a master instructing a number of senior pupils or "monitors," who then passed on their newly acquired knowledge to a larger number of pupils. Such methods were cheap, simple, and, it was widely believed, effective. They required a necessary emphasis upon facts, drill, repetition, mechanical learning, and ease of teaching. By 1820 there were 20 Lancastrian schools in the state of New York, where the system had official status until the middle of the century.

The monitorial system, although faulted, enabled a large number of children to achieve the minimum level of literacy on which future development could build. David Stow founded in 1834 the Glasgow Normal Seminary from which "trainers," as his graduates came to be called, went to schools in Scotland and many of the British colonial territories. In the United States, after an uncertain start, the Massachusetts Normal Schools founded by Horace Mann in the 1830s became a model for similar developments in Connecticut, Michigan, Rhode Island, Iowa, New Jersey, and Illinois. In England, churches and voluntary foundations were in process of establishing the first of the teacher-training colleges. Australia began the organized preparation of teachers in the early 1850s. The early inclusive pedagogic systems were falling into disfavor.

The problem arose of reconciling the teacher's personal need for education with his professional need for classroom technique. The work of Derwent Coleridge, principal of St. Mark's College, London, who admitted that he took his models not from the pedagogical seminaries of Germany but from the universities of Oxford and Cambridge, exemplified the attempt to introduce a larger element of general education into teacher preparation. Sir James Kay-Shuttleworth, founder of another London college, emphasized basic subject matter; he held that not merely the subjects of instruction, but also the methods of teaching the candidates, should be so ordered as to be in itself a preparation for their future vocation as teachers.

In Japan an ordinance of 1886 established higher normal schools for providing a four-year course for boys and girls who had completed eight years of elementary education. A French law of 1879 established a nationwide system of colleges for training women primary teachers (écoles normales d'institutrices). In Russia a statute on teachers' seminaries was promulgated in 1870; within five years there were 34 such institutions, with nearly 2,000 students. A further statute in 1872 provided for institutes to train teachers for the new higher grade schools that were beginning to appear in the larger towns. In Scotland, the universities of Edinburgh and St. Andrews established chairs in education in 1876. In the United States a large number of universities had by 1895 set up education departments, and in some of them the preparation of teachers for work in the schools was beginning to be combined with systematic study and research in education processes. Developments in American universities owed a great deal to the efforts of men such as Henry Barnard, who, as schools commissioner in Rhode Island from 1845 to 1849, stimulated a local interest in education that led to the creation of a department of education at Brown University. Barnard wrote an influential series of books on pedagogy and teacher education and later, as president of Columbia University, inspired Nicholas Murray Butler and others to found Teachers College in 1888. This soon became the foremost university school of education in the United States.)

The Indian Scene

The developments in the field of teacher education in India should be seen against their international backdrop. And also, before we deal with the recommendations of Kothari Commission and consider subsequent developments let us have a glimpse of its historical roots in this country first. Besides exporting the monitorial system from India that impacted teacher education movement in the U.K., the modern day Indian roots of teacher training could be traced back to the Danish missionaries who were the first to set up a teacher's training institution in Serampore (Bengal) in 1793.Theology-laced proselytizing-oriented Christian missionaries wanted India's poor, orphaned, lower-castes tribals, etc., to receive the fruits of their labor first. They therefore concentrated on elementary education area.

It may also be understood clearly that the need to train teachers during the rule of the East India Company arose for two reasons. 1. In order to cut costs of bringing in Europeans to man positions in commercial establishments the natives were taught in the schools opened both by the Missionaries for training native priests and the Company for low paid clerks. Training in both cases became necessary because the language and the culture of the natives and the Company differed radically; and, 2) a new culture needed both an orientation and acclimatization and the training offered an opportunity to come in close contact with each other. Additionally, who would prove to be better messengers of a new set up than the teachers who have access to all homes?

The first institution to be set up by the East India Company to train secondary teachers was opened at Madras in 1856. However, in its modified form Lord Elphinston had earlier tried the monitorial system in 1824 for training 26 teachers —12 in Gujarati and 14 in Marathi. The second institution was set up at Lahore in 1880. In 1886, the Madras Normal School was raised to the status of a college and was affiliated to Madras University. Even by 1902 there were no more than six training colleges and a few secondary training schools.

In between 1902 and 1966 lies India's struggle with its colonizers, an indigenous effort of several individual political and social leaders to make education available to its people and a strong desire to cover the hiatus between developed Europe and the underdeveloped Asia. It is in the intervening period between 1857-1882 that the three Presidencies had their three societies viz. Calcutta Book Society (1819), and the Native Book Society and the Madras School Society. These Societies were responsible for opening new schools with non-Native orientation both in textbook-content and teaching of a foreign language. All this led logically to the training of teachers on a very different footing. It is the natives who had come forward to learn a foreign language (the language of the new rulers and of their commerce) and desired to modernize themselves; therefore, it is these very people who should have come forward to expect training to match their efforts. The Court of Directors wrote to the Governor General of Bengal," by training, therefore, a class of teachers, you provide for the eventual extension of improved education to a portion of the natives of India, for exceeding that which any elementary instruction, that could be immediately bestowed, would have any chance of reaching." (Despatch, March 9, 1825 p.20). The Presidency towns were the first to have teacher training institutions, e.g. Madras had a Normal School in 1856.Around the time in 1882 when the Education Commission made its recommendations of a year's training for graduates to teach in secondary schools, the number of Normal Schools had gone up to 106 (1891 figures) and the total enrolment in them had touched the 3,886 teacher trainees mark. The training schools for mistresses had gone up to 8 (govt.), 4 (district & municipal); aided (18); unaided (7) with total number of pupils 793. The Commission (1882) approved the current teacher training programs for both elementary and secondary but envisaged a separate program for secondary distinctly higher in level and form and also method. The program should include, "an examination in the principles and practice of teaching.... success in which should hereafter be a condition of permanent employment as a teacher in any secondary school."

The 1904 Educational Policy Resolution of the Government made the intentions of the latter very clear:

"If the teaching in secondary schools is to be raised to a higher level, if the pupils are to be cured of the tendency to rely upon learning notes and textbooks by heart, if, in a word, European knowledge is to be diffused by the methods proper to it, then it is most necessary that the teachers should themselves be trained in the art of teaching." It is important to note that 'European knowledge' was considered superior to the 'native' knowledge and also only a certain type of European methods was suitable to imparting that knowledge. In a way this marks the beginning of regarding the rulers' knowledge and their teaching methods as superior to the ones already available in the country. It was for the first time a condition such as this was made compulsory that" a practicing school should be attached to each training college and that every possible care should be taken to maintain a connection between a training college and schools."

One must remember that there always was and shall always remain a gap between the Resolutions and the ground reality. The Resolution of 1913 (eventually under the modern system of education no teacher should be allowed to teach without a certificate that he is qualified to teach) and the Sadler Commission of 1917-19 emphasized the role of the universities in the training of teachers for the secondary education. As a result changes occurred in the provision of teacher education in the Indian universities. These changes were: 1) the starting of M.Ed. in the universities; 2) introduction of education as a subject for study at the B.A and Intermediate levels; 3) improvements in the physical facilities of teacher training institutions, and 4) setting up of an experimental high school to be attached to a training college.

Due to political upheavals in the country during the post-World War 1 period not much happened on this front. The Hartog Committee (1929) did make a few recommendations with regard to primary school teachers' training. It desired that the standards of education in primary schools must be raised, the period of training be increased; besides providing adequate staffs in the training institutions and an improvement in the service conditions of the primary teachers. The concept of in-service was introduced at this point in time.

The Central Advisory Board of Education adopted in its 1943 meeting the recommendations made earlier by the Committee on Recruitment, Training and Conditions of Service of teachers which had specified training teachers for pre-primary (2years); Junior Basic/primary (2); Senior Basic / middle (3 years); non-graduates in high schools (2) and the graduates in the high schools (1year).

The Sargent Committee (1944) repeated these recommendations in its report. By this time in-service teacher training in the form of short courses, evening classes, summer schools etc had become quite popular.

It may also be noted that the demand and supply position of trained teachers always showed a huge gap. This gap unfortunately has remained to be filled up till now.

In a free India the number of secondary teacher training institutions rose from 10 to 50; and to 993 in 1995.

However, by 1948 two types of agencies were involved in the provision of trained teachers: the State and the universities. The course content for both had by then become standardized. While the states continued to grant diplomas of teacher education (for instance, the department of education in U.P. offered a certificate course named L.T.), and the universities awarded their B.T. degrees. This duality of arrangements has led to numerous litigations between the agitating staffs and the State governments and until this day (2008) no change seems to have occurred in the situation. Lack of parity in both service conditions and salaries is currently responsible for the all-round deteriorating situation in this regard. The addition of self-financing institutions in the past couple of years has worsened the situation. There is hardly any move from any quarters to address this problem. This is also one reason that the teachers colleges continue to function in isolation. Several other issues continue to remain un-addressed. For instance, although there was an explicit requirement for a teachers' college to have a school attached to it but no one paid any heed to this stipulated condition. No research has tried to empirically prove that the theoretical content of teacher training is either adequate or meaningful. Similarly, although researches have not been able to establish that B.Ed. through correspondence is in anyway inferior to its face-to-face version, the former continues to retain almost an eternal question mark against its quality. We have gone on delivering judgments according to our whims and fancies. Similarly, it remains to be established what duration of teacher training is optimally suited but serious recommendations have been made whose roots lie in opinions rather than in research. We have had no qualms of conscience to look beyond our geographical boundaries to learn tricks of the trade. Besides, we have remained glued to the debates and research findings of the West to guide us in our efforts without bothering to be to be sure that physical conditions of a Nation have greater relevance in all dialogues than artificially generating desire for intellectual aping.

In between Mudaliar Commission and the Kothari Commission things as they stood are being recorded for ready reference and for historical relevance. There was in almost all States and Union Territories a crisis between the demand and supply of trained teachers. It is only for reference that we cite these figures. While in Tamilnadu 90% of the teachers in schools were trained in Assam the percentage of trained teachers stood at 16%. If Rajasthan had 57% of trained teachers in Uttar Pradesh and West Bengal it was difficult to find trained teachers for subjects like Physics, Chemistry and Mathematics. The situation of Delhi was also no better. There was an acute shortage of trained Science and Mathematics teachers.

According to S.N. Mukerji (Education of Teachers in India, S.Chand, 1968 p.455) in 1965 "the total number of teachers in the country was 1,909187 and they were employed in 579496 recognized schools. Of these 70% work in rural schools. The percentage of women teachers was 21.7 and of these 64.7 per cent worked in primary schools; 23.1% worked in middle sections and 12.2 % worked in secondary schools. Of the male teachers 62.1% worked in the primary sections, 22.8% in middle and the rest in secondary schools. 73.4 % teachers (female 77% & 72.5% men) were trained and the rest untrained. The additional requirement for trained teachers in the Fourth Plan period stood at 8 lakhs for the elementary and 2.15 lakhs for the secondary schools.

The diagnosis of the ailments in the area of teacher education revealed the following facts:

(a) The University Education Commission (1948-9) recorded "There is not much systematic research in Education going on in India today". It was particularly critical of the fact that ," too little time is given to school practice, too little weight is given to practice in assessing the student performance, and conditions of school practice are often unsatisfactory, sometimes quite grossly unsatisfactory." It was recorded that selecting a proper practicing school was a bit of a headache therefore it was recommended that only such schools should be chosen where perfect co-operation was forthcoming. This can happen only where the school Principals understood the need of teachers' colleges and were willing to help out. It was considered much better an arrangement where practicing schools were attached to teachers' colleges themselves.

(b) The Secondary Education Commission (52-53) observed, "However, excellent the program of teacher –training may be, it does not by itself produce an excellent teacher. It can only endanger knowledge, skills and attitudes, which will enable the teacher to begin his task with a reasonable degree of confidence and with the minimum amount of experience. Increased efficiency will come through experience critically analyzed and through individual and group effort at improvement. The teacher–training institutions should accept its responsibility for assisting in this in-service stage of teacher-training.

(c) The International Team (Ford Foundation, 1954 pp.28-29) recorded the following major defects: (1) Lack of integration in programs of teacher training for different levels; (2) In-sufficient co-ordination between the work done in training institutions and schools. (3) Inadequate conception of the role of training institutions for different levels and consequent inadequate staffing and equipment; (4) The domination of an external examination and its cramping effect on the training programs; (5) Inadequate provision for the training of certain types of teachers, viz. for Indian languages, of technical and other subjects such as agriculture, home science and commercial subjects; of craft; of art and music; of physical education.

(d) A study group set up on plan projects suggested, “As many of the existing 216 teacher training colleges as possible may be encouraged to develop into the new type of comprehensive teacher training institutions”

(e) An unpublished survey of the Teacher Education Department of the NCERT (1966) had revealed that out of 1,683 teacher educators working in the post-graduate training colleges in 1964-66 as many as 86 or 5.10 % were Ph.D.s 31.7% M.A., M. Ed.s and 41.09% were only M.A. B. Ed.s and some 7.61% were merely B.A.B. Eds.

f) The position is much worse at the elementary level, where the majority have had training in secondary teachers training colleges and have little or no experience at all of the elementary levels. Unfortunately, even now (2007) there is only a marginal change in the situation. The B.Eds, continue to be recruited for teaching at the primary level and untrained teachers at the university level are allowed to impart training for this level. The Courts of law have taken a dim view of the prevailing situation.

Baroda Committee Report also called Mukerji Committee Report had suggested that, "the Government of India should take early steps to set up by law an appropriate organization at the national level charged with the responsibility for planning, organizing supervising and financing teacher education. It may be called the National Council for Teacher Education; and, there should be constituted by a Statute in each state a State Council of Teacher Education, composed of representatives of the universities and the State departments of Education and other specialists."

A UGC Review Committee on Education (1966) reported, "There is at present a certain lack of agreement in regard to the principles and practices, incorporated in the program of study offered by various institutions in Education. The courses prescribed revealed considerable variations in regard to goals as well as the means for achieving them. Practices relating to admission, choice of the curriculum and type of research required of the students lack proper co-ordination. Such conditions make it difficult for various training institutions and departments of Education to make a real contribution to educational thinking and planning in the country." (p. 67)

In all, the country had in 1964-65 373 secondary teachers colleges of which 92 were Government colleges and the rest private and aided. The scales of pay differed from state to state and also between the Government-run institutions and the private or aided institutions. Lack of parity of scales and service conditions is reality even today. Since their salaries have remained low, teaching never attracted the best of human material. The Secondary Commission had therefore suggested, "We are convinced that if, the teachers' present mood of discontent and frustration is to be removed and education is to become a genuine nation-building activity, it is absolutely necessary to improve their status and their conditions of service." The overall situation in this regard has continued to remain dismal except in the centrally supported institutions.

In 1964-66 when an Education Commission headed by Dr. D. S. Kothari was appointed teacher education in India needed an in-depth study of the problems it faced and also the introduction of a series of far-sighted recommendations. Not only did the colonial past hung heavily on the system but the people also who functioned in the field seldom proved equal to the task on hand. Let us recall here that the Baroda group or / and the Indian Association of Teacher Educators—originally an Association of Teachers' College Principals, proved to be of immense help to the Commission for working in tandem to identify the problems this professional education faced. The Association had been trying to raise a few fundamental issues regarding teacher education program from time to time. In a way some of their principal concerns were paid attention to by the Commission. This by itself was fairly gratifying. Additionally, as a reward for their concern for the cause of Teacher Education the Association's President was co-opted as a member on the UGC's panel on Teacher Education. In brief, we present a summary of the points the IATE had raised from time to time.

(1) The Association wanted the quality of teacher preparation should be improved. Toward this end, the Association

wanted National Council of Teacher Education should be constituted with similar arrangements that were being followed at the State level.

(2) The Association felt concerned for the training of primary and elementary teacher training program and demanded stopping the B.Eds from getting employed for teaching elementary level classes for which they were neither trained nor did they have any preferences. The Association pointed out, "The B.Ed. degree has been designed 'to meet the requirements of secondary education classes and does not cater to the needs of elementary education classes at all." (Elementary Teacher Education, NCERT, 1965, PP. 1501)

(3) They were the first to point out that four–year teachers' colleges were welcome additions and the experiment should be seriously conducted. The Association also proposed that the minimum strength of a Teachers college for elementary teachers should be 200 and 100 for secondary student trainees and the practice of teaching should be paid maximum attention. It would be a better idea if the practice teaching were done in schools that looked kindly at this most essential component of teacher training.

(4) The most perceptive recommendation of the IATE was to integrate teacher education program and to keep it all under a single umbrella-like arrangement. This, the Association believed should take care of the most of the problems this branch of professional preparation faced.

Without going any further into the history of teacher education in the country, we could consider the major findings of the Commission and its recommendations and compare the same with today's ground reality and try to make out a case for radical changes needed to improve things as they exist.

In my opinion if only the recommendations of the Kothari Commission were implemented we might never have reached the stage that we find ourselves in and the only way out left for us to adopt is to revisit the Commission and its recommendations. Let us read the Commission's text first:

In its chapter 3 titled Teacher Status the Commission raised first the issue of Remuneration or Teachers salaries. The first point they noted was that despite all efforts "the net results achieved have not been adequate." The Commission noted that teachers' salaries differed from State to State and within the State also. "At the school stage, however, the problem is more difficult because the desirability of introducing national scales of pay at this stage is itself challenged." Therefore, they recommended," the remuneration of teachers under different managements should also be the same and all teachers having same qualifications and the same responsibilities should have the same or at least similar, remuneration and conditions of work and service." In principle parity in work should result in parity in salaries.

The Commission noted that in higher education also there were wide variations in salaries of teachers and the working conditions too differed greatly. The Commission argued, "it is essential to adopt the principle of parity in remuneration, and simultaneously to prescribe the same qualifications for teachers in all types of schools and to introduce similar machinery for their recruitment." The Commission made it clear that it was opposed to the policy of frequent transfers of teachers and wished that the teachers be given 'academic freedom'. They exhorted the State governments that the principle of parity should be adopted as a State policy. Where Public Service Commission did not appoint teachers; the situation needed considerable improvement. Therefore, the Commission wanted the qualifications of teachers to be identical with those working in Government colleges and institutions. For overseeing this, the management committees should adopt and function according to the conditions laid down in the Model Act Committee.

At the school level too the salaries of teachers needed immediate upgrading and substantial increases.

In the case of retirement benefits both at the higher level and at the school levels two sets of recommendations were made: a) As an interim measure, and b) on a permanent basis. Before uniformity was achieved in this area the 'triple benefit scheme' already in force in several states should be implemented across the nation. The private schools should also be brought within the ambit of these recommendations and be forced to adopt proper terms and conditions of service. The Commission was very particular that in the tribal areas too good teachers be appointed and their working conditions improved.

Two more points were raised in this regard and improvements suggested.

(1) 'On the lines of the scheme recently approved by the Government of India for Joint Consultative machinery and compulsory arbitration for Central Government employees, we recommend the constitution of joint teachers' councils in each state and union territories.

(2) The Commission wanted "professional organizations of teachers fulfilling certain (desirable) functions and having a responsible and representative body of members be recognized by the Central and State Governments."

In brief, the Commission not only wanted the status of teachers to improve, their sagging morale to lift but they also wanted the means to improve their societal conditions by enabling them to merit it. The only means to do so would be to institute National Awards for schoolteachers. They recommended 500 awards annually for the primary teachers and 200 for the secondary teachers.

In chapter 4 the Commission went into the problems Teacher Education faced. The Commission defined the significance of this program as: "A sound programme of professional education of teachers is essential for the qualitative improvement of education. Investment in teacher education can yield very rich dividends because the financial resources required are small when measured against the resulting improvements in the education of the millions." The Commission was conscious of the fact that in the absence of proper training the teachers will tend to perpetuate the traditional methods of teaching. It was necessary they learnt 'new and dynamic methods of instruction'.

They listed major existing weaknesses in the system because barring exceptions the quality of training institutions remained either mediocre or poor. "Competent staff are not attracted; vitality and realism are lacking in the curriculum and program of work, which continue to be largely traditional; and set patterns and rigid techniques are followed in the practice teaching, with a disregard for present day needs and objectives." Therefore, a comprehensive program of improvement was urgently needed in teacher education, which was discussed under the following heads.

1. Removing the isolation of training institutions by bringing them into the mainstream of the academic life of the universities and by building up closer relations with the schools and between the training institutions preparing teachers for different levels;

2. Improving the quality of training programs and training institutions;

3. Expanding training facilities;

4. Making adequate provision for the continuing professional education of all teachers; and

5. Creating appropriate agencies, both at the Center and in the States, for the maintenance of standards in Teacher Education.

The Commission was dismayed at the general trend in India of trying to identify education with pedagogy. Because of this peculiarity it is mostly taught in the teachers training institutions. The fact on the other hand was that 'education has developed considerably as a social science and a separate academic discipline. The realization that education is an instrument of change— social, political and economic—is having far-reaching implications, not only as an intellectual discipline of great scientific and philosophic import, but for other disciplines as well. Therefore, the first recommendation of the Commission was," that in view of its increasing scope and importance,' education' should be recognized as social science or an independent discipline. The next recommendation therefore had to be the one that enabled 'education' to become an elective subject that should be introduced at the undergraduate and postgraduate stages on the lines detailed below:

(a) The courses in undergraduate education should give an orientation in three broad areas—sociological, philosophical and psychological foundations of education. The contributions of great educators, comparative education and a study of some of the current educational problems could be included in the course.

The most significant part of the recommendation was the defining purpose of introducing education as an independent discipline, which covered 'the interrelationship of education with national development in all its aspects.' This quote also explains the reason behind Commission's reported title: 'Education and National Development.' A wide choice should be given to a student to combine this discipline with other subject such as mathematics, behavioral sciences, natural sciences etc.

(b) At the post-graduate level, an M.A. degree in Education, to be taken after the first degree in any subject, should be introduced. In addition it should be possible for a student to combine education with one other subject selected from a wide range in the humanities and the sciences. To begin with, this may be given to students who offer it and who agree to teachers after the completion of the course.

(c) In all these courses —undergraduate or postgraduate—a minimum of teaching practice—should be obligatory just as laboratory work is compulsory part of the study of sciences. It should be possible for a student who has taken these courses, to become a teacher, after a period of internship and, if necessary after some in-service education provided through summer institutes.

It was not very surprising to see that the Commission wanted this course to be introduced by the UGC in a few selected universities. In each selected university, a Department or an Institute or preferably a School of Education was to be established to develop research and training programs in collaboration with other disciplines. The main functions of such an institution would be (1) to conduct courses in professional education for different categories of teachers; (2) to provide extension services to a few institutions of teachers education at all levels and to assist them to grow; (3) to organize summer institutes and in-service programs in subject content as well as in professional education; (4) to work in close collaboration with a few schools of all types with a view to developing research and evolving better curricula and techniques of teaching; and (5) to promote research in education, especially with an interdisciplinary approach.

All these recommendations were intended to enhance the value and also enrich teacher education programs, but the most crucial of them was to see that a "practice was adopted to appoint eminent professors as part –time professors in the schools of education to explain new developments in their fields and the manner in which they will affect education at the school stage." The idea behind this recommendation was a) that it will attract talented students to study teacher education in combination with other subjects without a commitment to becoming teachers; and b) a few of them might eventually feel disposed to becoming teachers. In any case this closeness to education by scholars from other disciplines was bound to enrich education.

Breaking isolation from schools:- To break down isolation from schools, every training institution should be required to guide neighborhood schools and their staff in planning their work and in using improved methods of teaching. The idea behind this kind of extension work was that it would bring about an improvement in training college activity. Therefore, the Commission recommended each training institution should have an extension department that looked after the activities of pre-primary, primary or secondary as an essential part of the teacher education program. The other method suggested by the Commission was to activate 'old boys' association. And the third method was to make student –teaching a comprehensive internship in which the trainees participated in all the professional activities of the school both in and out of school.

The Commission also wanted that to break the isolation of institutions training primary, pre-primary and secondary teachers to come together and for this end in view the status of pre-primary and primary level teacher training should be raised to the collegiate level. This will help breaking down of isolation, raising the status of the training institutions and enhancing the effectiveness of the programmes.

In order to prevent the sudden rise in the high costs of setting up these institutions the Commission wanted all this to happen in a phased manner spread over several years. The transitional strategy to be adopted was to comprise: (a) the establishment of Comprehensive Colleges; (b) up-gradation of primary and pre-primary institutions; and (c) the setting up of State Boards of Teacher Education that may function as bridges between the universities, the government institutions and the National Association of Teacher Education. It is this Board that shall prescribe standards for training colleges; bring about improvement in the curricula, prescribe conditions for the recognition of training colleges and arrange periodical inspections, offer consultative services to the institutions; ensure the competency of teachers coming out of the training colleges, and prepare plans for immediate and long –term development of teacher education.

The next problem the Commission addressed related to the quality of Teacher Education per se. It declared, “We attach the highest importance to this program of qualitative improvement.” They had found the existing programs to be largely traditional, rigid and divorced from the realities of schools and existing or proposed programs of educational reconstruction.

The Commission suggested reorganization of the same on the following lines:

Reorganization of subject knowledge: The Commission wanted to avoid confusion regarding this aspect of reorganization with a program of study of subjects not offered at the college stage, and neither with the mere imparting of additional information in the subject. Instead it should be a carefully planned content course, which would include a study of fundamental concepts and their implications for the school syllabus, and of the textbooks and growing source materials to assist teaching at the school stage. In terms of time it should be 20% of the time.

Duration of the course: At the primary level the course should be run for two years. However, at the secondary level the course should remain limited to one year that is the number of working days, in this case should be increased to 230 from the existing 180-190. Since in some institutions this kind of extension has yielded good results this scheme should be extended uniformly to all teacher-training institutions in the country.

It further suggested that this re-organization be done in collaboration with competent university departments and, where necessary, with science and arts colleges doing post-graduate work. And this was to be done after having prepared a detailed scheme involving not only their staffs but also the use of laboratories and libraries. Similar courses like the ones suggested above should be provided by staff members, who hold a Masters degree, in collaboration with the staffs of arts and science colleges. However, re-orientation courses in subject-knowledge should be closely related to the special techniques and methods used in teaching the subject concerned.

Integrated Courses of General and Professional Education: While assessing the Kurukshetra Experiment, the work done by the Regional Colleges of Education and in one Rural Institute, the Commission concluded that the criticism of these courses such as which says that there is "no evidence to show that the products of these integrated courses are better than teachers who have first taken their degree and then completed their professional education thereafter;" is not valid. However, considering the expenditure involved for running such courses are such that only a small fraction of the required number of teacher could come out of the system." Therefore, it was better to concentrate on the 'improving the professional one-year course following the first or second degree.' The Commission clearly did not favor multiplication of institutions like the RCEs because of certain very valid reasons like expenses involved, lack of motivation for competent people to join such institutions etc.

The Commission wanted the avoidance of crowding the course content. It desired concentration on the need to coordinate and integrate different courses and to root the entire curriculum in Indian conditions. They pin-pointed two major defects in the system: (1) inadequate research on problems under Indian conditions, which explains why teachers take recourse to foreign theories and explanations while discussing Indian problems; and (2) the corollary to the first reason cited is the absence of original books in education by Indian authors. Absence of such books is more glaring at the primary levels.

The next problem the Commission addressed pertained to, "Improving methods of teaching and evaluation." In the opinion of the Commission "methods of teaching and evaluation in training institutions are extremely important. Hence, the suggestion: (a) an attempt should be made to develop the student-teachers maturity through contacts, experience, study and discussion: (b) time should be found to orientate students' attitudes to the significance and possibilities of the profession that they have chosen; (c) a number of new techniques and methods are being developed rapidly in the advanced countries, such as use of radio, television and films etc in classroom instruction.

The Commission drew attention towards the need to improve the nature of examinations in the training institutions. They clearly wanted internal examination to form the necessary plank of the improved evaluation system.

The other problem toward which the Commission drew attention was practice of teaching, which according to them should be arranged in two phases. While the first phase should consist of acquainting student teachers with schools' working conditions, use of libraries, laboratories etc the second phase was to comprise actual teaching in the natural school conditions stretching to at least eight weeks.

The Commission was conscious of the need to offering specially designed courses for the variety of specially challenged students who needed highly specialized instruction.

The next in the series to draw the attention of the Commission was the issue of 'revision and improvement "of the curricula for all stages and types of teacher education. The Commission found nothing amiss in the current teacher education curricula but in the area of preparing Primary School teachers and others they favored "the subject matter presented under various heads in theory to be of direct relevance to the task that a teacher is called upon to perform in the school" and that "they should be taught in an integrated manner." In addition, the teachers need courses, which will help them to build up' a proper perspective of life, of our cultural heritage and of problems and aspirations of the nation as well as human culture and civilization in general.'

In the case of secondary teacher education curricula too the Commission wanted 'elimination of irrelevant matter' and to 'relate to the teachers' responsibilities and to Indian conditions, problems and studies.' Clearly, they wished the teachers to understand and appreciate "the nature of forces—social, political, religious, economic and technological, which are tending to transform modern Indian society." It is at this level that the teacher-trainees be provided specific training in constructing diagnostic and achievement tests.

The teacher–training program should be organized in the spirit of a community enterprise. The Commission admitted that it was not possible to 'offer a complete training to meet all anticipated situations.' But the curriculum and programme of activities to be followed in training colleges must be such as will meet the requirements of national system. This is to be the primary task of the State Boards of Teacher Education and the standing Committee of the UGC on Teacher Education.

The Commission found "the existing courses for Masters' degree in education lack effective and thoughtful direction and that they are mostly ornamental except for service in a training college". The existing courses are not closely linked with professional needs at a higher level not do they have the depth and intensity necessary for the study of education as an academic discipline. They appear to have grown out of the B.Ed. courses without any clear idea of their purpose.

The Commission made a few observations on post-graduate studies in education. A post-graduate degree course should include (1) core courses to provide the student with a perspective for the study of education and educational problems and to familiarize him with scientific ways of studying them (2) courses in areas of specialization related to some field such as educational planning and management, teacher education, guidance and counseling, educational evaluation, or psychological foundations of education, (3) the study of methodology of research, and (4) a dissertation. The organization of courses should be flexible and allow for a wide choice to suit different purposes.

It was pointed out that a postgraduate degree is not a necessary qualification for teaching profession. In fact, researches have revealed that the caliber of the candidates who come for this degree generally lack in it. It was also pointed out that offering postgraduate degrees is not an essential function of teacher training. Only where the staff is competent and the needed facilities available such a provision should be made.

The Commission took note of a finding that had revealed serious shortcomings in the qualifications of the staff employed in the teachers' colleges. Therefore, the Commission recommended that there should be a substantial increase in the output of Ph.Ds, M.Eds and M.As in Education. In exceptional cases where lack of professional qualification prevents a competent person from other Discipline this condition may be relaxed.

The Commission regretted the shortcomings in the subject-knowledge of those that came for joining teaching profession. It also came to light that in several States it was not binding that a person should teach only that subject for which he was qualified or had a degree. Even at the university stage facilities for teaching of such subjects like Geography etc. are inadequate and prospective teachers who come forward to earning degrees or diplomas are far from being very bright. They also noted an acute shortage of teachers of mathematics, science subjects and

English. It was because of these deficiencies that up-gradation of subject-knowledge at the secondary levels becomes very difficult. "The obvious long-range solution is to improve standards at the degree level and to raise the remuneration of teachers so that adequate number of competent individuals came forward to joining this profession." The additional recommendations constituted (a) that as a rule the universities should insist that one who had not studied a subject at the level of first degree should not be allowed to earn a Masters degree in the subject. (b) In those cases where someone came forward to teach a given subject without an essential qualification, h/she must be asked to take a special course in that specialization. (c) The output of postgraduate degree holders in school subjects should be increased; and (d) efforts should be made to bring in good second class or first class degree holders to come and join teacher training courses.

The Commission felt concerned at the lack of Hostel and residential facilities for the students and the staff. At least the minimum facilities in this regard may be provided in teachers' colleges.

The Commission learnt with dismay both about the working conditions, qualifications of teacher-trainers, their salaries and competencies etc. to be much worse than those prevailing in the secondary level teachers training colleges. The number of graduates working at this level was only 0.3%, secondary /undergraduates 10.1%, and not completed secondary education stood at 89.6%.

The Commission recommended that the new appointments should be given to only those that have had at least 10 years of schooling. Emphasis should be laid on getting the present staff become more qualified. It was recommended that primary teachers should not be grouped together because of the great diversity in their qualifications. At this level tuition fees should be abolished. The facilities for teacher training at this level should be greatly enhanced. Since teacher qualifications vary from State to State expansion of enrolments should be carefully planned. For instance, Madras, Kerala and the Punjab already have a very large number of qualified teachers; therefore there is a need to match facilities with their requirements.

While preparing plans care should be taken to expand full-time facilities, provide additionally part-time facilities, offer correspondence programs in the State Institutes of Education; start evening part-time courses and also try to clear up the backlog.

The other recommendation related to the size of the institutions offering training courses. "With a view to ensuring economy and efficiency, training institutions should be of large sizes." While for the two-year courses the intake should of 240 and for the secondary stage it should be 200. And when a new institution is being set up the minimum size should not be less than 400. However, the most significant recommendation related to opening of primary teachers' institutions. These were to be opened in the rural areas and the practice teaching conducted in the nearby localities. To break isolation of teacher training institutions the major recommendation was for the IITs and agricultural universities to open wings for teacher-training programs. It was assumed that "programs of this type will give a status and a broader basis for the training of teachers. Besides, it will also help to give education an orientation to agriculture and industry."

The other major recommendation related to "the professional preparation of teachers in higher education." The Commission regretted that there was until then no provision for the 'professional initiation of a university teacher. A lecturer is generally expected to take on his full load of teaching work—

and sometime even more—from the first day of his appointment. He generally receives no initiation into his duties and no re-orientation to his profession.' Additionally, 'he is given no time for adaptation and no chance to watch the good senior teachers taking their classes.' He has no prescribed opportunity to study the syllabus, plan lectures, consult the head of his department or other senior colleagues about them, or to study the techniques of seminars and tutorial classes. It has therefore resulted in the pointless tradition of 'giving lectures' and dictating notes.

The incalculable loss involved in this unimaginative approach can and should be avoided. The tradition in India has been to regard training college lecturers as unnecessary. But the fact is, 'in most highly skilled professions — and education is certainly one—training is regarded as an essential qualification.' The Commission appreciated the scheme of summer institutes but desired that since they were not the complete answer a system has to be evolved in which the newly appointed teachers get time and opportunity to acclimatize themselves to the institution. The teachers were encouraged to attend the lectures delivered by senior teachers in their subject areas. Besides, all universities and colleges have to organize orientation courses for a few weeks each. The Commission wanted that in some bigger universities or a group of universities," these activities may be placed on a permanent footing by establishing something like a staff college where teachers from all affiliated and constituent colleges as well as university will be brought together for orientation, discussion, seminars, workshops, etc."

The last and perhaps the most important point concerned the need for an organization that looked after the standards of teacher education in the country. It was necessary both for coordinating the variety in courses, conditions of work, and quality of teacher turn out. For this job the advice was to the

UGC to look after these concerns through a Joint Standing Committee with NCERT on Teacher Education after co-opting a few representatives from various bodies both national and state.

The Commission defined the job of the Standing Committee in areas that related to all aspects of teacher education, general and professional at both undergraduate and postgraduate levels. The idea was that this body will develop and raise standards of teachers' colleges, co-ordinate and improve standards of teacher education per se; grant funds to these colleges; arrange periodic inspections; and see that teacher education institutions were supported financially.

The closing part of the Report of the Commission recommended, "the Government of India will have to provide funds liberally to develop teacher education programs on the lines recommended. Some of the programs that need emphasis are: the upgrading of training institutions for primary teachers to the university standards, improvement programs of training institutions at all levels, correspondence education; in-service institutions; and the establishment of training institutions of large size."

Following the 'Commission' Report a Committee of Members of Parliament was setup in 1967 to prepare a draft of a statement on the National Policy on Education, which covered most of the major points recommended in the Commission's Report; such as teacher training should be brought within the broad stream of university life and to end isolation of training institutions from schools should be ended. Each State was then expected to prepare and implement, on a priority basis, a plan for expansion and improvement of teacher education at all stages. They also made a mention of revolutionizing education per se by adopting new techniques and methods of instruction.

Meanwhile, between the years 1967-71 the UGC sent three delegations to the USSR for studying evening and correspondence courses. Correspondence had in the meantime become popular in China too. Meanwhile, a Steering Committee of the Planning Group on Education (1968) had also endorsed the Education Commission's major recommendations on teacher education.

National Education Policy came in 1968. It acknowledged not only the importance of teachers and their education in the system but talked of their academic freedom; emphasized in-service education and broke new ground in several other aspects. While the Education Commission had been very enthusiastic about the integrated courses like the one of Kurukshetra University and of the Regional Colleges of Education, but sadly enough it was no more possible to continue with their programs. The reasons were many. If the RCEs had to wind up their technology-based courses, the multi-purpose scheme itself had flopped in view of 10+2+3 making the courses at the RCEs redundant. All this had forced the Government to re-think about the integrated scheme and indeed to bid goodbye to the idea itself.

In the history of teacher education 1973 is fairly important. A committee had considered the extension of one-year teacher training to two years but this suggestion was not agreed upon for several practical reasons. In the meantime the NCTE also came up.

Let us now recount the tale of what has happened in these past 40 years since 1968 NPE. In the year 2008 the position of the teacher education is no better than it was when the Education Commission had looked at it. The Government of India cannot be blamed wholly for what has happened. The fault does not lie with the institutions that the Government created under various regulations and an Act of Parliament. Instead, the responsibility for the deterioration in the situation lies squarely with the university departments and colleges of education for their lack of vision, their love for extra-mural interests and the conspiratorial behavior besides clique-formations resulting in mafia-like activities unmindful of the ground reality that one day their actions will have a serious bearing on the school system itself. They indulged in the very same activities against which the Commission had made adverse remarks such as unplanned proliferation of institutions of teacher education and their commercialization. The blame for all this cannot be laid at the doors of the politicians alone who today under the present day NCTE dispensation chair all regional committees and who invariably have one or more B.Ed. colleges of their own as well. While the entry of the politicians and businessmen into the lucrative trade of teacher training sounded the bugle for the destruction of the system, the teaching community headed by their professorial class was seldom found wanting in co-operation with these interests. A draft curriculum framework brought out by the NCERT clearly mentions on p.8.

"Teacher education institutions suffer from isolation at both levels: the school as well as from the centers of higher learning. Often in schools, the method of teaching curricula and various other requirements are different from those advocated and implemented in teacher education institutes. As a result schools consider teaching education institutes as alien and not a space for 'realistic' professional development of teaching. The teacher education on the other hand, merely fulfill the formality of completing the prescribed number of 'lesson plans' with little concern for preparing teachers for constantly demanding and fluid classroom situations. The rapid commercial mushrooming of private 'teacher education shops' has further accentuated such divides."

After reading this one can well see that neither the UGC and nor the NCTE who are vested with power and authority ever acted with alacrity and determination and nor are they even now willing to take steps that might stem the rot at some point.

In the UGC's domain a few universities took lead in setting the rot in motion. If M.D. University was responsible for leading the commercialization of B.Ed. degrees, the Annamalai University literally finished the sanctity of teacher preparation; and the rest has later on been completed by the IGNOU. Other universities like H.P.University too did not lag behind. And all this happened under the vigilant eyes of the UGC. Alas! The UGC has always betrayed Nation's trust. It never learnt to earn public respect.

The well-known names among professors of education equally failed to keep their reputations intact. It is these professors who participated in the racket of approving self-financing institutions in the name of the NCTE and brought down the reputation of the newly created apex body from day one. It is these professors who served as Inspectors and decision makers in the NCTE collaborated with business interests and eventually made Anand Sarup committee to record the sordid truth.

Almost simultaneously the judgment of Honorable Supreme Court on the Chhattisgarh scandal (private universities, which the National Knowledge Commission proposes to support) brought out into the open how business interests could dominate higher education by opening universities in rented two room locations, with or without any permanent staffs. But for the intervention of the Supreme Court things in higher education too would not have remained as they are today. If this could happen to higher education where the business and politics could reduce higher education to a state of mockery, what can one expect from teacher education dignitaries whose respect was always qualified?

We have thus far seen that teacher education was virtually infested with problems and the suggestions too to overcome these were seldom found wanting either in good intentions or sagacity. For instance, the Baroda group had suggested the formation of a body like the NCTE and their suggestion included its nomenclature too. In fact, the Commission had accepted most of the recommendations made by this Group and even acknowledged the source. Long before the NCTE Act, the NCTE itself had started functioning as a result of Government of India's Resolution (1973) from the NCERT's department of teacher education. In its initial avatar the NCERT- based NCTE prepared a curriculum for B.Ed. and produced several meaningful reports besides gathering statistics regarding teacher training. In fact, numerous clauses for the Act itself were initially drafted in the NCERT. Before the contribution of the NCERT and its departments passes out into the oblivion, its initial history should be recounted in detail.

Besides the NCTE's curricular frameworks in 1978 and 1988, the other documents on the subject appeared in the form of the report by the National Commission on Teachers I (1983-85); the UGC curriculum (1987); National Policy on Education 1968 and 1986 and the eight Five-year Plans. The POA (1992) is yet another document in this field. All these documents had their relevance, but the general criticism of the hiatus between suggested improvements and their actual implementation has been ascribed to the theoretical nature of the recommendations. An NCTE document (titled: Policy Perspectives in Teacher Education p. 53) says, "Opportunities need to be given to the practitioners to interact with 'theoreticians' and with the involvement of both, to work out details, evolve field-feasible practices, try them out systematically and convey the entire set of experiences to others in terms of their comprehensiveness, impact potential and relevance. Willing institutions may have to be identified and encouraged to try out varied curricula at different stages without the constraints of having to prove compatibility with existing teacher education programs in regard to the substance, organization and certification procedures." While this document does touch upon the cause of the malaise that afflicts teacher education, it says nothing about the anomalies that have continued to afflict the system per se. For instance, while this is supposed to be a 'skill' area, it continues to be taught as an information-based domain. The NCTE does seemingly regard teacher education as part of higher education but even the CTEs have only M.A. B. Eds as teaching faculty who are allowed to take B.Ed. classes and the NCTE regretfully connives with this lacuna.

Be that as it may, the Framework (1978) that considered all the three aspects of teacher education program viz. pedagogic theory, working with the community, and content-cum-methodology and practice teaching, including practical work was the result of the joint effort of the UGC's Panel on teacher education and the NCTE. It also delineated the entry conditions, duration of the courses and the like for each stage separately, viz. pre-school; elementary school, high school and higher secondary.

The most meaningful thought can be discerned in the following few lines: of the Framework (1978), p. 9.

"If ever teacher education were to be successful in analyzing its goal into a series of concrete and hierarchically graded cognitive and socio-national tasks to be accomplished by the teacher–trainee, then it would have found not only a meaningful but also an indispensable man-making process."

We need hardly to go into this any further beyond saying that no one had until then bothered to analyze the goals of teacher education and neither had anyone graded its cognitive and social goals with any degree of clarity. Interestingly, while this Framework accepts explicitly a skill-based approach to teacher education, and lays stress upon task-oriented methods and techniques, it is the institutionalized NCTE body that forgot all about its own past recommendations.

In the Teacher Education Curriculum Framework (1988), which apparently had the benefit of the National Policy on Education (1986) and the NCERT' s National Curriculum exercise (1988) derived its rationale to sum up its goals: " Thus the future teacher will be a competent professional, skilled teacher like the one he always has been expected to be, but this would now mean that he will be an effective communicator, a designer and user of learning resources, a learning facilitator and an effective participant in community life."

Framework (1988) suggested the following components common to all stages of teacher education," (1) Foundation courses; (2) Stage-relevant specialization and (3) Field work / practicum The Framework (1988) was certain that while this course structure would remain popular, there was a possibility that integrated structures would also be given a trial, which many include two-year pre-primary level training after 10+; three-year integrated after 10+; and 3year after 10+2 +3 for the secondary classes. The teacher also stood defined in terms of the whole process the transaction of which would enable the achievement of "a goal of preparing an effective teacher rather than making him a knowledge seeker from any one theoretical viewpoint (perspective), or even a set of theoretical standpoints separately." As against the current practice of collecting "too many areas of knowledge and several activities"; it should lead to a very integrated view of what is presented in terms of content knowledge, skills and their application.

The other attempt to improve matters was made by the UGC through a Curriculum Development Center in the department of education of Kerala University. An extract from its Framework reveals the intentions. "We teach all schools of philosophy and leave students to link the practice with a particular philosophy. Very often they form no link or only a weak link." The fact is our trainees "need psycho-pedagogy and not psychology." Of all the innovative programs, the RCE experiment was linked the most. Even the Teachers Commission I (1983-85) had favored it. The Acharya Ramamurti Committee also endorsed this recommendation.

It would be pertinent to remember that most of the educational developments that followed the recommendations of the Education Commission (1964-66) drew inspiration from them. It is another matter that the ground reality continues to be depressingly disappointing. Of the several institutions that took birth after 1966 the most important of them all is the coming up of the National Council for Teacher Education. Since it all took its final shape in an Act of Parliament, let us consider first the Act itself presented and passed on Thursday, December 30, 1993 / Pausa 9, 1915.

Firstly, an Act of Parliament is a well-thought out document, therefore technically it provides ideal conditions for work. Secondly, Acts of Parliament create institutions that are of a permanent nature and seldom need amendments. Thirdly, these institutions develop fairly comprehensive policies that avoid creeping in of anomalies either in day-to-day functioning or in the achievement of long-range goals. We shall examine the NCTE Act against this backdrop. Now the Act itself:

"An Act to provide for the establishment of a National Council for Teacher Education with a view to achieving planned and coordinated development of the teacher education system throughout the country, the regulation and proper maintenance of norms and standards in the teacher education system and for matters connected therewith."

This Act constituted the Council with Chairperson, Vice-Chairperson and the Member Secretary all appointed by the Central Government and quite a few ex-officio member and others from the field such as professors of education, experts in all areas of teacher education such as pre-primary, secondary etc and a few M.P.s and State officials.

While the Act defined conditions of work of all its functionaries, it did not lay down any qualification or the criteria for the selection of either the Chairperson or his deputy or even of the Member Secretary, but is very specific about their disqualification. The membership of an individual can be terminated on various grounds detailed in section 5 including clause (e), which says that if, "in the opinion of the Central Government it is likely to affect prejudicially the discharge by him of his functions as a Member"; or, in the opinion of the Central Government (he) has so abused his position as to render his continuance in office detrimental to the public interest.

Thus far no one has been penalized for the activities indulged in, that fall under these provisions. Even the Anand Sarup Committee's expose also did not merit any dismissals or removals.

Chapter III defines the functions of the Council, which begins by stressing upon the need to conduct surveys and studies relating to various aspects of teacher education and publish the results thereof.

Make recommendations to the Central and State governments, Universities and the UGC and recognized in the matter of preparation of suitable plans and programs in the field of teacher education; besides its functions include laying down qualifications of teachers to be employed in schools; lay down norms for any specified category of courses or training in teacher education; lay down guidelines for compliance by recognized institutions, and for providing physical and instructions facilities, staffing pattern and staff qualifications; lay down standards in respect of examinations leading to teacher education qualifications, criteria for admission; and lay down guidelines regarding tuition fees and other fees chargeable; and lastly, take all steps to prevent commercialization of teacher education.

For the performance of its duties mentioned in the last part of this section the NCTE was authorized to "cause Inspections of any such institution, to be made by such persons as it may direct, and in such manner as may be prescribed." The Council shall communicate to the said institution its views and the executive authority thereof shall report back the action taken on the recommendations made thereof;

Chapter IV of the Act lays down conditions for the recognition or otherwise of the teacher education institution but here no requirement of the practicing school has been mentioned.

The powers of the Regional Committees are such that reduce ordinarily the central body as no more than a figurehead or a mere coordinating agency. As a de facto body the Regional Offices could perpetrate any mischief it plans because the central body has in extreme cases (chapter V. 21(1) subject to the clause28 in chapter VII) over-riding powers; otherwise the ROs function as the 'eyes and ears' of the Council. This section does not limit the powers of the Universities to multiply teacher education institutions because it implies that they shall not cross the boundaries of sagacity. The ground reality is however considerably at variance with their assumed behaviour.

Chapter V defines the Bodies, Constitution and their functioning, besides a few powers and the job requirements.

Chapter VI deals with Finance Accounts and Audits i.e. preparation of budget for income and expense accounts as laid down for any office for the inspection of the Audit and Report to the Government.

Chapter VII titled Miscellaneous defines the limits to the Council's powers and also contains a Clause 30(1), which accords the Central Government the authority to 'supersede (wide section 29) the Council wide a Notification' to this effect and can also extend the period of its supersession.

One should note clause (31.1) of chapter VII, which clearly defines the extent of the powers the Government could exercise should it so desire, because it could 'by notification in the Gazette, make rules to carry out the provisions of the Act.

In essence, the MHRD presided over by the Union Minister has the last word in the functioning of the Council. The rest is a mere facade.

However, the last part of the Act (32,2.d.) does talk of norms, guidelines and standards in respect of qualifications of the teacher, courses, training, and the examination leading to the degree in teacher training.

There can be no one better qualified to make an observation on the functioning of the NCTE than an ex-Secretary, MHRD who also looked into the complaints against the mal-functioning of its Regional Committees and its achievements in Bihar.

"Everybody knows the hopes with which the National Council of Teachers Education was set up. Nobody has evaluated how it has been functioning. Unfortunately, it is even more of an island than the UGC or the NCERT or NIEPA. Some years back when the issue of core curriculum was such a central point of debate, inquiries revealed that NCERT and NCTE had not got together to discuss whether (and how) the curriculum could be handled by the community of teachers.

"A couple of years back, a random sampling of Teacher Training institutions showed that neither the NCTE nor the Universities' departments of Education sent out any meaningful literature to either the Teacher Training Institutions or to the teachers. Since its inception, NCTE has not been able to ensure the publication of a Journal of Teacher Education on a regular basis. As long as Teacher Education remains so badly neglected, how can one hope that an average school would be able to ensure either the empowerment of children or even the prevention of such a high rate of drop-outs at almost every stage of education" Anand Sarup Committee report on NCTE, 2001.

What is the way out?

Things fall apart, the center cannot hold;
Mere anarchy is loosed upon the world,
The blood–dimmed tide is loosed, and everywhere
The ceremony of innocence is drowned.
(*The Second Coming*)

W.B. Yeats

Before we deal with the suggestions to improve the system we must remember that, had the UGC played its role efficiently and kept institutions like the Annamalai and the Rohtak Universities within control, things would not have come to this pass. In fact, there would have been no need to have yet another body like the NCTE and the mushroom growth of teachers' colleges could have been easily prevented. As we cannot go back into the past and rectify things it is still possible to remove anomalies and make the system both honest and transparently functional.

In the past couple of decades there has been an exponential growth in the teacher education institutions* and especially after the coming in of the self-financing institutions it would appear that virtually the floodgates for opening new institutions have been opened. Teacher education has taken on the shape and texture that it is impossible to recognize anymore. Until these colleges came to be opened there was at least seemingly some (not much, though) honesty around. None would have believed that teachers too could be so dishonest or manipulative. But these days it has become rare for a teacher either to be honest or be non-manipulative. For one reason or the other they are minting money. NCTE has come into being only for these manipulative, cheating teachers. It is these individuals who become NCTE experts or Inspectors. It is these Inspectors who have contributed immensely in bringing a bad name to the organization that trusted them so much.

While the Kothari Commission had laid stress on removing disparities in the system and wanted avoidance of anomalies either in terms of status, qualifications, salaries or the structure, today what we find is that both anomalies and disparities have come to rule the roost. What is missing is a concerted, cohesive and well-thought out plan to remove all the distortions in the system. Numerous examples can be cited about the confusion the contradictions in the policy decisions of NCTE and the UGC have created. For example, while the UGC would like all teachers teaching B.Ed. should have similar qualifications, draw similar salaries and become part of the higher education, the NCTE is uncertain about it and refuses to take steps to rectify the situation A recent field study by (TERG) for the NCTE has brought out the fact in clear terms that no one is serious about teacher education program. The institutions like the DIET, SCERT, etc. for instance, that have come up in the past couple of decades and function under the State control rarely follow norms for appointing teachers and have no clear-cut transfer policies. The MHRD does not send the grants in time and the programs that need money in advance are therefore seldom conducted with any degree of seriousness. The entire system smacks of lethargy and lack of vision.

Similarly, the question of relaxing qualifications e.g. the clearance of NET / SLET or obtaining of Ph.D. etc. is not very clear. (See, appendix B for details on the conflict between the UGC & NCTE).

The political party in power manipulates education system the way it so desires and the instrument in this regard is the Minister, MHRD. No political party in Free India has been found 'Not Guilty' thus far.

Still a lot can be done to improve the situation.

To start with the first requirement is to make employers apply the rule strictly that no B.Eds are appointed to teach primary classes. Also, B.Ed will not be appointed even as Headmasters in Primary School. This decision has been delivered in the M.P. by its High Court. Let us hope NCTE does not go against this judgment

Following the Education Commission's Report no one should be allowed to open or continue having a B.Ed. college unless it has its own practicing school. Those that do not have a school may be encouraged to open one. This would additionally help bridge the gulf between the required number of schools and the illiterates in the neighbourhood.

If these two recommendations of the Education Commission are implemented with some degree of seriousness, it is possible to improve educational standards all around.

The other points to consider relate to understanding the nature of teaching. We must remember that a teacher plays a variety of roles in the classroom and also vis-à-vis society. We need teachers who know how to communicate; have reasonably developed reading habits, and those that feel socially and morally responsible toward their wards. It is against this backdrop we have to offer prospective teachers courses of study so that our classrooms are provided teachers; who at least partially possess necessary competencies. Our present day teacher education curricula refuse to offer us any hope. Even as it is the researches find that teacher trainers have very poor reading habits.

The answer to the question posed above lies in introducing radical changes in the NCTE's approach to the problem. The NCTE should acknowledge and declare like the Kothari Commission Report did, that teacher education is a skill area and not an information domain. The first rule it should uniformly apply is to declare that no teacher training college or department shall be able to run an institution unless it has a practicing school attached to it. For the time being a relaxation may be given to those who submit an affidavit that they have free access to a school, which will not disallow practice of teaching in their classes. Numerous defects and deficiencies in teacher education that one comes across these days shall disappear automatically.

The second is to apply the criterion of relevance on the prescribed curricula. No piece of information or a skill could be taught unless its relevance for a practicing teacher in the classroom has been demonstrated. In fact, now is the time when NCTE could play its leadership role. It should commission empirical studies the results of which may be considered for the prospective curricula for incorporation. This is one way to improve matters.

We should re-state what the Indian Education Commission had already acknowledged. Teacher training is a skill area. There is absolutely no need to clutter this course of study with mere information. The tragedy of information is that it is dated and its long-term utility highly dubious. Therefore, conduct surveys and undertake massive empirical studies so as to discover the requirements of teachers in classrooms—do they need some technique or mere information? Thereafter, we should develop a body of knowledge about the existing reality. Teach relevant skills and not mere information should be the aim of teacher training. Theoretical researches are good but the ones that resolve problems whether they come in the form of answers to questions or relate to future requirements should become the guiding principle. For instance, look at the work being done by the NGOs. It is these people who come out with brilliant solutions to almost un-resolvable problems. They innovate, reduce time in teaching but are still able to manage to meet day to day challenges; and then compare the same with hundreds of Ph.D. in Education whose total contribution is nothing more than accumulated, highly confusing verbiage, whose relevance or utility either for policy making or improving class room practices is a big zero. Their researches in fact do not develop in them any liking for academic work or even a positive attitude towards them per se either. It is doubtful if until now we have found a single solution or even an alternative to our practical problems with their help.

Therefore, it is high time we changed our track in this connection. The curriculum for the B.Ed. should drastically change. The NCERT has prepared one for the NCTE. It is expected that in a nationwide discussion on this curriculum framework it has come out that this framework is meant to defend and continue RIE programs as well as the fact that verbiage hide more than they reveal. Meanwhile, the NCERT has already produced textbooks based on its revised school curricula and has taken action on its own teacher education curricula.

In my judgment the time has come to accept that as an alternative to the existing program one should start teaching skills of communication; meaning of gestures in classroom; offer assistance in developing command on good language; when and how to put stress on a syllable, word or a sentence in communication; skills in reasoning and logic more especially lateral thinking; disabuse the minds of teachers against prejudices, define a prejudice—racial, caste, color, language, sex etc and discuss techniques of eradicating the same; and in the process teach meaning of life and how to develop a philosophy of life and not schools of philosophy; and, teach classroom management and ideal behavior and not theories or models of teaching This is only an example. Teach nothing that is either irrelevant or is a mere theory. Teaching to learn is always superior to teaching to store. Therefore, teach and improve the process and not merely the product.

Whether or not we should have Norms?

Yes, norms are necessary. But only those that relate to cognition. The building or infra-structural norms are for engineers and one must put this question first: How is the infrastructure related to levels of learning? Answer this question and then move forward. Thereafter define cognitional requirements Similar other questions too come immediately to one's mind. But the solutions can be simple. Only one has to try and identify them.

Involve those NGOs that have a proven record of achievements and innovations. Let them also test each theory that one introduces. In terms of social acceptance teachers also need a few qualities. These qualities are teaching skills or teaching competencies. If it is possible to prepare teachers on these lines then our job is fully done.

Appendix A

Statewise Number of Diets

State	*Number of Institutes*
ANDHRA PRADESH	29
ARUNACHAL PRADESH	6
ASSAM	17
BIHAR	10
CHHATISGARH	7
DELHI	9
GOA	1
GUJARAT	23
HARYANA	13
HIMACHAL PRADESH	12
JHARKHAND	5
KARNATAKA	20
KERALA	14
MADHYA PRADESH	38
MAHARASHTRA	29
MANIPUR	11
MEGHALAYA	3
MIZORAM	2
NAGALAND	2
ORISSA	13

(Contd.)

(Contd. Appendix-A)

State	*Number of Institutes*
PONDICHERRY	1
PUNJAB	12
RAJASTHAN	31
SIKKIM	1
TAMILNADU	29
TRIPURA	5
UTTAR PRADESH	55
UTTARANCHAL	9
TOTAL	407

STATEWISE NUMBER OF PRE-PRIMARY INSTITUTES AND THEIR INTAKE

State	*Number of Institutes*	*Intake*
ANDHRA PRADESH	2	95
ARUNACHAL PRADESH	1	50
BIHAR	1	150
CHANDIGARH	2	140
DELHI	30	1585
GUJARAT	31	1441
HARYANA	4	200
HIMACHAL PRADESH	1	50
JHARKHAND	1	50
KARNATAKA	17	920
KERALA	27	1077
MADHYA PRADESH	8	350
MAHARASHTRA	5	235
MEGHALAYA	1	40

(Contd.)

(Contd. Appendix-A)

State	*Number of Institutes*	*Intake*
ORISSA	2	100
PUNJAB	5	250
RAJASTHAN	11	600
TAMILNADU	5	250
UTTAR PRADESH	26	1306
UTTARANCHAL	3	190
TOTAL	183	907

STATE-WISE NUMBER OF SECONDARY INSTITUTES AND THEIR INTAKE

State	*Number of Institutes*	*Intake*
A & N ISLANDS	1	90
ANDHRA PRADESH	321	35641
ARUNACHAL PRADESH	2	160
ASSAM	42	3450
BIHAR	11	1460
CHANDIGARH	4	540
CHHATISGARH	48	5150
DAMAN & DIU	1	60
DELHI	33	3338
GOA	4	400
GUJARAT	174	16310
HARYANA	44	4600
HIMACHAL PRADESH	33	3525
JHARKHAND	35	3550
KARNATAKA	337	33660

(Contd.)

(Contd. Appendix-A)

State	*Number of Institutes*	*Intake*
KERALA	166	18090
MADHYA PRADESH	261	25920
MAHARASHTRA	236	22370
MANIPUR	5	680
MEGHALAYA	4	400
MIZORAM	1	120
NAGALAND	3	280
ORISSA	15	1248
PONDICHERRY	24	2492
PUNJAB	120	13805
RAJASTHAN	135	14810
SIKKIM	2	200
TAMILNADU	174	18734
TRIPURA	3	350
UTTAR PRADESH	686	66595
UTTARANCHAL	49	4700
WEST BENGAL	34	3287
TOTAL	3008	306015

State-wise Number of Elementary Institutes and their Intake

State	*Number of Institutes*	*Intake*
A&N Islands	1	60
Andhra Pradesh	187	10500
Arunachal Pradesh	5	245
Assam	21	1270
Bihar	29	1670
Chandigarh	2	150

(Contd.)

(Contd. Appendix-A)

State	*Number of Institutes*	*Intake*
Chattisgarh	21	1420
Daman & Diu	2	100
Delhi	30	3230
Goa	2	150
Gujarat	260	14059
Haryana	66	5905
Himachal Pradesh	24	2475
Jharkhand	21	1260
Karnataka	744	40788
Kerala	188	8823
Madhya Pradesh	87	4716
Maharashtra	427	21293
Manipur	11	550
Meghalaya	5	334
Mizoram	2	220
Nagaland	3	160
Orissa	66	5456
Pondicherry	27	2400
Punjab	29	2050
Rajasthan	82	5117
Sikkim	2	90
Tamilnadu	315	22520
Tripura	5	624
Uttar Pradesh	199	16840
Uttaranchal	10	950
West Bengal	20	980
Total	2893	176408

Appendix B

(CONFUSING NOTIFICATIONS)

The University Grants Commission (UGC), New Delhi on the recommendations of the Mungekar Committee constituted by the MHRD has come out with a Notification on 14 June 2006, which stipulates the following as the eligibility criteria for becoming a Lecturer in a University or its constituent and affiliated colleges:

1. NET in the subject concerned
   Or
2. Ph.D. in the subject concerned
   Or
3. M.Phil. in subject concerned

However, an M.Phil in the subject concerned shall be eligible to teach only the Undergraduate classes.

In juxtaposition to these provisions is the Gazette Notification issued by the National Council for Teacher Education (NCTE), New Delhi of 28 December 2005 (**Published in Part – III, Section 4 of the Gazette of India Extra-ordinary as Number 12 on 25 January 2006**) vide which the relaxation in NET/SLET/PhD. has been granted in the following manner:

"The relaxation would be considered only as a temporary measure for a period of 3 years permitting regular appointment subject to confirmation after the appointee becomes eligible on clearance of NET/SLET/Ph.D etc." The same notification further states as follows:

"Relaxation of the requirement of NET/SLET can be made only by the competent authority in the National Council for Teacher Education."

The clause 9 of the Notification is as follows:

"In respect of teachers already working and requiring exemption from NET/SLET before issuance of this notification, proposals for seeking relaxation from the requirement of NET/SLET shall be submitted to the headquarters of the National Council for Teacher Education on the prescribed format along with the approval of the competent/appointing authority, within two months of the publication of the notification."

Now, these two Notifications issued by two regulatory and statutory bodies both framed by respective Acts of Parliament give rise to the following issues:

1. Is it the NCTE or the UGC or both which are empowered to grant relaxations in the qualifications of the teachers in the Universities, and their constituent and affiliated Colleges?

2. How can there be the dichotomies in the relaxations granted by these two regulatory bodies? Whereas the UGC's Notification mandates that a prospective teacher in a University or a College shall have either qualified the NET in the subject concerned or have a Ph.D. or an M.Phil. in subject concerned.

   The NCTE's Notification considers a simple Post Graduate in Education i.e. M.Ed. to be eligible for a teacher in the institutions of the Higher Education.

3. Whether the Universities shall go by the UGC's Notification or the NCTE's Notification at the time of granting affiliations to the Teachers' Colleges? Whose Notification shall now prevail?

4. Is not the NCTE accepting this fact now that when no such relaxation was available from its own side even then

there were the people who had been appointed in the Teachers' Colleges who had not qualified the NET/SLET or did not have the degree of Ph.D. in Education awarded to them before December 2002?

Rajasthan Patrika, dated 18 March 2006) that the Central Administrative Tribunal reports that B. Ed. as ineligible for Primary Teacher's post.

The Principal of IASE Bikaner (it is a Government IASE) is Mr Chagan Lal Verma. He is M.A., and B.Ed. It is a different thing that M.Ed. course is being provided in this IASE. Moreover he is also the Nodal Officer of all IASEs and CTEs in Rajasthan. This reflects that neither the Guidelines issued by the MHRD way back in 1987 nor the Norms laid down by the NCTE are being followed.

The Times of India (July 10, 2006) on its page 11 i.e. TIMES NATION has carried a Notification issued by Maharshi Valmiki College of Education, Geeta Colony, Delhi-31. It is a College of the Govt. of NCT of Delhi. This Notification in fact is a corrigendum in the qualifications announced earlier for the posts of Lecturer in Education (Methods of Teaching Hindi, Economics, Physics, Chemistry, History, Sanskrit). This Notification now has been issued in light of the new or revised qualifications as announced by the UGC in its Notification of 14th June 2006. I copy below the Notification as it has appeared in the TOI.

"Reference Advertisement dated 31.03.06 in daily "Times of India" for six different posts of Lecturer in Education (Methods of Teaching Hindi, Economics, Physics, Chemistry, History, Sanskrit). "NET shall remain the compulsory requirement for appointment as Lecturer for those with Post-graduate degree. However, the candidates having Ph.D. Degree in the concerned subject are exempted from NET for PG level and UG level teaching. The candidates having M.Phil. Degree in the concerned subject are exempted from NET for UG level teaching only." **Those who have not applied earlier may do so within seven (7) days of the publication of this notice.**

Dr. PRABHJOT KULKARNI"

Now, this Notification is not in consonance with the Norm laid down by the National Council for Teacher Education (NCTE) but is in consonance with the UGC Notification. I seek the following information and clarification under the provisions of the Right to Information Act 2005:

1. Is Maharshi Valmiki College of Education, Geeta Colony, Delhi-31 correct if it goes by the UGC Notification and not by the NCTE Norm?

2. Will the NCTE get different persons' candidature considered for these different posts of Lecturers in this College when the applicants are not NET qualified in Education, do not posses Ph.D. in Education, and also do not posses M.Phil. in Education?

3. Will the NCTE allow a College of Education which is recognized by the NCTE itself not to go by its own Gazette Notification of 28.12.2005 (Published in Part – III, Section 4 of the Gazette of India Extra-ordinary as Number 12 on 25 January 2006) vide which certain relaxations were granted in the qualifications for the posts of Lecturers in the Colleges of Education?

4. Whose rules, norms and regulations must a College of Education recognized by the NCTE follow - NCTE's or the UGC's? - especially in a situation where there are contradictions in the rules, norms and regulations?

In an NCTE publication titled 'Envisioning Teacher Education in the 10th Plan and Beyond' (NCTE Document 2003/71) the 4th Chapter is "CENTRAL GUIDELINES FOR FINANCING STATE SPECIFIC PLANNING AND IMPLEMENTATION IN THE 10TH PLAN" contributed by Ms. Rashmi Sharma, Director, Department of Elementary Education and Literacy, MHRD, Govt. of India.

The bases of my writing this application under the RTI Act 2005 seeking information from you are some of the relevant contents of this article. I wish to draw your attention to these contents because a strict adherence to them by the Government of Rajasthan should be insisted upon as hitherto the Norms and Guidelines pertaining to the qualifications and pay-scales of the teachers (i.e. of Principals, Professors, Readers, Sr. Lecturers, and Lecturers) of the IASEs and CTEs have not been adhered to in spite of their clear mention in the earlier Guidelines issued in 1987.

The following mentions in the above-referred Chapter need immediate attention.

"Central Government funding to Teacher Education will be conditional to the States putting in place certain basics, such as appropriate recruitment and placement policies of teacher educators, role definition of teacher education institutes, their links with schools, etc. Thus placement of appropriate faculty, maintenance of buildings, supervision and support from the state level would be pre-requisites for central funding."

"Basic conditions to be put in place by States":

"It is recognized that goals cannot be achieved till a facilitative environment is created. High quality work is unlikely to ensure from teacher education institutes that are badly staffed and structured. Therefore, funding of State activities will be contingent on States fulfilling the following basic conditions identified by the Working Group.

- Appropriate recruitment and placement policy for faculty in teacher education institutes.

The above provisions in the Guidelines reflect the thrust of the MHRD on the recruitment and placement of appropriate faculty. In Rajasthan, the teaching staff is not appointed as per the norms of the UGC and the NCTE. Neither are they paid the salaries as per the pay-scales as prescribed by the UGC. We have information that the IASEs and CTEs in other States follow UGC norms in recruitment and the payment of the salaries. The examples that immediately come to mind are of IASE, Jamia Millia Islamia, IASE, Department of Education, Ruhelkhand University, Bareilly (UP), etc. When the staff there is within the University how is it that in Rajasthan the teachers working in IASEs and CTEs are under the School system though all these Colleges are affiliated to different Universities.

Even the letter conveying the approval of the **Government of India (issued vide letter No. F.3-17/87-TE (Desk) dated 29th March 1988 of Ministry of Human Resource Development (Department of Education))** states in its conditions (Para 5 (v)), "............Pay scales of these posts will be determined by the State Government, keeping in view the recommendations contained in the Guidelines in this regard." These recommendations are as follows:

"The most important corollary of this would be that posts of Lecturers, Readers, and Professors in these institutions will necessarily have to be manned only by persons satisfying mutatis mutandis, the eligibility criteria laid down by the UGC for these posts,

for the 'General' category of colleges (i.e. those imparting instruction in Science, Humanities, Commerce, etc.)"

Contrary to the above, the posts of Lecturers, Readers, and Professors in these institutions (i.e. in IASEs and CTEs) in Rajasthan are being manned by persons satisfying the eligibility criteria laid down by the Rajasthan government which is not in consonance with the criteria laid down by the UGC.

Further, the Guidelines stated that:

"Holders of the above posts in CTEs / IASEs must not merely by recruited in accordance with rigorous qualifications as above, but should also be given parity with their counterparts in the 'General' colleges in the matter of pay scales. In certain States, Lecturers, Principals, etc. of STEIs are not placed in the UGC or 'General' college pay scales but on par with State Govt. officers like Assistant Directors, Dy. ./ Jt. Directors etc wherever such prevailing scales are poorer than the ones suggested above, the State Govt. may attempt to increase them and bring them on par scales applicable to 'General' colleges. Wherever such up-gradation is done, Central assistance will be available to the extent of State's/UT's additional liability created on this account, until the end of VII Plan period."

Just contrary to the above the teachers working and teaching in IASEs and CTEs in Rajasthan are at par with the State Government officers like Assistant Directors, Dy./Jt. Directors, etc and their prevailing scales are poorer than the one suggested under the Guidelines i.e. the UGC pay scales. The posts of Lecturers in these IASEs and CTEs are at par with the Vice-Principals of the Government Senior Secondary Schools and any Vice-Principal of such a school be posted in Government IASEs as a Lecturer.

Since **the Government of Rajasthan** does not want to create a fresh cadre for their IASEs and CTEs as such the IASEs and CTEs of non-government sector (though three of them receive grant-in-aid from the State government and one of them has also been upgraded as a deemed-to-be University) are also being treated not within the College system but within the School system.

The following information was sought under the RTI Act 2005:

1. Is the Department of Elementary Education in the MHRD aware that the teachers working in the IASEs and CTEs in Rajasthan are in the school education and as such not at par with the University and other 'General' College teachers?

2. If the Department of EE in the MHRD is not aware of this fact then was it never observed or checked by it before the releasing of the Grants to the State of Rajasthan if the conditions laid down in the Guidelines issued by it were being followed by the State Government or not?

3. Does the Department of EE in the MHRD accept this fact that the entire thrust of the Guidelines framed and issued by it is now lost and the money spent on the IASEs and CTEs in Rajasthan has not resulted in the quality improvement of the in-service teachers and the teacher education in Rajasthan?

4. Does the Department of EE in the MHRD accept and believe that by not getting the Government of Rajasthan adhere to the provisions of the Guidelines issued by the MHRD and even by continuing releasing the Grants to the Government of Rajasthan since 1987 or 1988 till date

for the programmes under the IASEs and CTEs a great loss to the Public Exchequer has been made and the money thus spent has been squandered?

5

Information Technology and the Digital Divide

R.P. Singh

Contemporary education is witness to far greater changes in both the curricula and methods of instruction in the past couple of decades than in the past couple of centuries put together. Not only we have larger numbers of peripatetic teachers, but also we have tremendous variety of institutional mobility. The tools of instruction also appear to have changed in very many ways. In a way all this constitutes globalization. Globalization per se as a concept and practice both are not new to an Indian. Indian literature both ancient and modern is replete with references declaring the world as being a single large unit and most of the time we also practice the idea literally, which holds that "the entire human race is but one family". What greater proof for this practice could one offer than to point out the presence of millions of Indians living abroad. Indian religions too have unhesitatingly been unanimous about endorsing this view. Since this concept is embedded naturally in the Indian psyche we seldom face problems on that score. We could easily cite numerous hymns and verses from Indian literature both ancient and modern to endorse the statements made here.

The theme implies that if material conditions remained unchanged the process of globalization, the world would continue to remain homogeneous and basically equal. The fact is that thus far we have neither knowledge nor experience of any society that could ever qualify to be called either equal or homogenous. To me it looks as though the Divine intention itself was not to create a world that would ever be so boring as to be either equal or homogenous. What perhaps is possible is to offer an infrastructure that makes equity an achievable object. There are several philosophical systems that decry equality but support equality of opportunity. In brief, they are all for equity. The tragedy with this almost universal desire is that it is a mere formulation of a concept and not a roadmap for an action plan.

It would be advisable not to overlook the fact that equality is an unachievable goal. In reality it is a virtual impossibility to succeed in this direction. It is both sensible and relevant to say that it is also an undesirable value because no society could ever function with that kind of an impossible reality. All of us are aware that there are two types of constructs—the real and the ideal. An Ideal is what inspires one to work hard and compete and the Real is wherein one shall always fall short of the Ideal. Life acquires meaning by our efforts to bridge the distance between the Real and the Ideal. What the ancient Indians were talking of (vasudaiva kutumbkam) will forever remain an ideal construct even as our dream to have equity practiced in today's world becomes a virtual reality. This diversion was intentional lest we overlooked the main issues involved here. The main issue for debate in my opinion is whether or not globalization is bound to lead to digital divide. My contention in this regard is that globalization will have its impact in several other ways rather than create inequality. No society was ever equal and neither it is likely to ever become so. Inequality is embedded in the nature of society itself.

The other points relate to poverty and co-existence of numerous hierarchical layers of social and economic existence and progress. At no point of time in Indian history have we been free from the misery of poverty. Indeed, the very progress of our society has been totally unrelated to the reality of prosperity. Certain classes or castes in India have traditionally been rich at the expense of others. One needs to consult the history of our society to get an idea why prosperity has been praised by so many. Praise is invariably reserved for the rare and the exclusive. We take for granted what is readily available. Riches or fortunes are destined to be in the hands of few. We must also acknowledge the reality that Indian society is inherently and basically unequal. It is not merely the caste that divides us all but the political system that has grown overtime too has acquired a vested interest in poverty. For instance, what would happen to the Left parties if for some reason India came out of its vice-like grip of poverty? Not only will they become irrelevant because they will then lose the constituency they have thus far cultivated, they will also be forced to look for some other ideology to survive. Without going into a diversionary mode let me state here that it is not true that we have waited for countless centuries to see that as a society we should get divided digitally, we have been and are a remorselessly divided society with or without any innovation or scientific advancement. Therefore, what happens now will in no way be worse than what the existing reality is. In other words, what I am saying is that the so-called digital divide is likely to do us some good instead of something unimaginably worse.

I refuse to mourn the absence of equality in our society. The gadgetry involved in modern-day information technology and its mastery and command by a few will have on those means of transmission compares well with the inventions of gunpowder or paper or the wheel etc. Every time something new comes it takes time to percolate down to deliver its benefits universally. The ones who are fortunate or intelligent enough constitute the vanguard of prosperity. In the process they are likely to accumulate unprecedented power either of expertise or the riches. This is some kind of universal law. Nothing new is likely to happen even now. The very concept of digital divide is contextually misplaced and ill conceived.

What we must note at this juncture are a few important facts about India's new class structures. We already know that India is caste-ridden and is afflicted with regional biases with plenty of tribal dominated areas. Still, in order to describe this social reality we might as well use the well-known terms Lord C.P. Snow used some five decades back to describe the British society. India lives on in numerous concentric circles of parallel societies with minimum number of communication channels open for any kind of dialogue. The English speaking/knowing urban elite knows nothing or very little about the majority of non-English speaking / knowing Indians. Thanks to oil boom the non-English knowing India's unskilled workers suddenly hit the jackpot. They built big mansions from their earnings abroad in remote villages and are even willing to invest in education for children. The classical example of this trend can be witnessed both in Kerala and Bihar. The results of their monetary investment have not been universally beneficial.

India's traditional urban elites continue to have a vested interest in the preservation of the once discredited 'British heritage.' Therefore, they read, speak and think in English and attend the same clubs as their erstwhile rulers did. They have their exclusive schools, which charge heavy fees just 'to maintain standards.' Their children go to Mission Colleges and join All-India services or the multinationals. They marry within their class and should the caste also match they then have the best of both the worlds.

India has accepted the West as a model for modernization. In the process, Indians have ceased to be prejudiced against the use of English language, which during India's struggle for freedom symbolized foreign domination. Indeed, after independence, the mastery of this language has been instrumental in creating a class of rulers who are imposing Western ideas and institutions on the non-English knowing people. If this has led to a social division of Indian people, it is helping a few to attain a good deal of prosperity at the cost of others. More so now that India has joined the WTO regime, the information technology has come to rule the roost. The implications are there for all to witness. There was a time when the Tatas and the Birlas were the richest Indian business families. Today they stand outclassed by Premji & Co.

The majority of the non-elites join government run/grants-in-aid/charity/ municipal schools. These schools may teach the same curriculum as the elites do but here the teaching is carried on in Hindi or some regional language. And from then onwards starts the discriminatory process eventually leading these children to a future of becoming second-grade citizens. Couple of decades back there was always a possibility that few of the non-elites will crossover the dividing lines and join the mainstream elites. This is going to become unlikely now.

Educationally the great urban-rural divide has become glaring in most parts of the country. The villages do have their schools—a vast majority of them being single-teacher. The reaffirmation of faith in the Sarva Shiksha Abhiyan by the UPA notwithstanding the village school retains, by and large, its 'community center character' where all varieties of social functions including political meetings and gram panchayat sessions are held. During summer and winter breaks its buildings serves as a barat ghar (wedding-hall) or when the teacher is away which is fairly frequent the students indulge in free-for-all games. The seriousness with which the government issues fiats for running these schools is truly a mockery of commitment where even the barest minimum facilities and climate for teaching happen to be non-existent. Expecting such schools to bring up rural / tribal children ready for a highly competitive world is surely a cruel joke on an unsuspecting crowd.

All Indian cities are facing an explosion in population, a large chunk of which consists of migrant, unskilled labor, adding a shanty township each month. Since they serve as vote-banks for the ruling party before every municipal or parliamentary election, they are regularized. The inhuman conditions in which these people live are seasonally improved and gradually municipal schools start appearing as pleasant surprises in an otherwise bleak surrounding. However, what is shocking is that villages are gradually becoming slums—where the landless laborer and the old cobbler or blacksmith finds it difficult to survive. With the arrival of technology in Indian farming and the formation of co-operatives in states like Maharashtra, Gujarat, etc. rural life has become quite comfortable for the landowners even when their landholdings are not very large. With television covering most of the country's population and pocket radios available almost universally the complexion of social life is gradually getting urbanized even in remote corners of the country. While the banking services have now become available in majority of rural pockets, hoards of urban entrepreneurs have landed up in rural areas in search of cheap labor and land for their industries. The mushroom growth of plantation societies has more or less established that Indians can smell economic benefits from miles away. What I am trying to say is that even without much effort Indians seem to be happy with their socially divided existence and highly discriminating school system. If one added the presence of antiquated religious schools to this list, the divisions already in existence are arguably not dependent on any digital phenomenon.

Human progress since the most ancient times could be defined in terms of its march towards providing basic necessities of life to all. This progress should be seen as an effort to be creating conditions under which one could claim to have some dignity attached to human life. These efforts are definable in terms of one's ability to earn one's livelihood and to live in reasonable safety. One should also see that even this modest goal has remained elusive in majority of the cases. The enlightened people are interested to see that human past does not extend beyond the pages of history read in school days. Probably this seems to explain the choice of the present sub-theme.

Let me now take up seriatim the problems of globalization vis-à-vis India as they cover areas beyond the territorial boundaries defined in terms of nation states. However, most of the problems arise when one talks in terms of Nation-States. Several thinkers believe that since all humans belong to the same race the world must be treated as a common habitat. The political process that led to the formation of Nation States has now to be put into the reverse gear. To that end we have several world organizations trying to iron out political and other varieties of rivalries. Besides, it makes economic sense to fight jointly when faced with a common yet strong enemy. Modern technology and innovations and research are an expensive business. The EU experiment therefore should be seen against that background. This holds out a hope that something like this may have to be evolved in the Asian region too. The SAARC strikes immediately as our response to the EU model.

We can see that Europe has gradually overcome the concept of nation states and is becoming socially and economically a cohesive, competitive society. Others who had thus far not refused to be part of it are queuing up to join in. A typically Christian Europe is being wooed by a dominant Islamic country like Turkey to become a part of it. The very concept of Europe trying to unite is the result of an American threat to dominate and weaken it. Besides being a question of survival and acquiring the ability to stand up to American challenge, the economic reasons have far out-weighed other considerations. Educational system is getting defined to become an instrument of the latest warfare. Research is getting due weightage and the mobility of scholars is being deliberately promoted and encouraged. Without going into details let us accept that EU is emerging as a model of future trans-border arrangement to meet challenges of WTO and the IPR etc. The march of globalization is largely livelihood-driven. An eminent economist of Indian origin Jagdish Bhagwati is responsible for the establishment of World Migration Organisation and editorially The Times of India (Dec.18, 2002) has called for India to opt for Akhand pluralism. This is one reason why India has started looking invitingly toward the East. Recent moves to get gas via Bangladesh or the trading co-operation with China are all examples of our acknowledgement of the changing reality. The world has somehow been unsuccessful in retaining sacrosanct the existing political arrangement called the nation-states and its boundaries and even the national languages are gradually losing out to the dominant world language. We have today numerous world organizations promoting socio-economic unity and almost all governments are a party to their running. Even in India the dominant languages that help one to migrate from one state to another are either English or Hindi. Therefore, one must acknowledge the reality of local and regional languages losing out to politically dominant and economically helpful languages. DTH might prove to be a great help in retaining and even enriching regional and local languages. But one is unsure about their bright future.

India is unfortunately facing tremendous internal ethnic and religious problems. These biases and disagreements are preventing it to become a Nation with a mission. The tribes, castes and regions besides multiplicity of languages are preventing it to put up a combined fight on any front. Consequently, it is the 'minority groups' among Indians that are reaping all the benefits, but as a nation we are losing out on almost all fronts. We not only lack imaginative leadership but the irresponsible behavior of the majority of our legislators gives us no hope for a better future.

Microsoft entry defines "globalization as a concept that encapsulates the growth of connections between people on a planetary scale." Globalization involves the reduction of barriers to trans-world contacts. Many believe that through it people become more able—physically, legally, culturally, and psychologically—to engage with each other in "one world".

The same write-up continues to say:

"Global connections take many forms. For instance, jet aeroplanes transport passengers and cargo across any distance on the planet within a day. Telephone and computer networks effect near-instantaneous interpersonal communication between points all over the Earth. Electronic mass media broadcast messages to world audiences. Countless goods and services (such as Nissan cars and Club Med holidays) are supplied to consumers in global markets. Moreover, some articles (including much clothing and electronics) are manufactured through trans-world processes, where different stages of production are located at widely dispersed locations on the Earth. The US dollar and the Euro are examples of currencies that have global circulation. In global finance, various types of savings and credits (for example, offshore bank deposits and Eurobonds) flow in the world as a single space. Many firms (for example, Exxon), voluntary associations (for instance, Amnesty International), and regulatory agencies (such as the World Trade Organization) operate across the globe. Climate change (so-called "global warming") and stratospheric ozone depletion are instances of anthropogenic (that is, human-induced) ecological developments that unfold on a planetary scale. Finally, people experience global consciousness, in as much as we define the realm of our lives in trans-world, planetary terms."

With globalization the world as a whole also becomes a social space in its own right. Thus global connections entail a different kind of geography. Whereas other social contexts are territorially delimited, global relations transcend territorial distances and territorial borders to unfold on planet Earth as a single social space. In this sense globalization might be characterized as the rise of "supra-territoriality". Whatever it may mean to others for an Indian it is not easy to eliminate the significance of localities, countries, and regions. Nor does the spread of trans-world connections abolish territorial governments or dissolve territorial identities. The global coexists and interrelates with the local, the national, the regional, and other dimensions of geography.

Globalization has also not encompassed all of humanity to the same extent. In terms of territorial location, for example, global networks have involved the populations of North America,

Western Europe, and East Asia much more than other parts of the world. In terms of class, global finance has been a domain of the wealthy far more than the poor. In terms of gender, men have linked up to global computer networks much more than women. This kind of gender bias was somehow only to be expected.

Needless to say, this unevenness of globalization has important implications for social power relations. One could easily witness the impact of power relations. People with connections to supra-territorial spaces have access to important resources and influence that are denied to those who are left outside. In this regard, some commentators have 'deplored "global apartheid", as manifested in the so-called "digital divide" and other inequalities. Others have objected to a "cultural imperialism" of Hollywood and McDonald's in contemporary globalization. Since the mid-1990s such discontents have provoked a so-called "anti-globalization movement" marked by regular mass protests against global companies, the International Monetary Fund, and other prominent agents of trans-world relations.

Conceptually globalization may be easy to define but its practices remain both unclear and indistinct. Semantically or even contextually too it fails to be distinct. Perhaps it has its origins mainly in business and operationally it borrows its attributes and the definition of its characteristics from the models offered by the MNCs. Politically it has its bases in the power equations. Each country is today defined in terms of political power it has or does not have. It would appear that the USA has the monopoly of defining who will do what and how. Deviations from that definition are not permitted. Those that defy her authority to do so face armed intervention. When applied to education it would mean IPR and world rating of institutions. By implications it means that standards of educational degrees will have to be defined in the international context. The analogy is available in the world of patents of drugs or industrial products. The copyrights and patents give certain privileges to their original creators/ innovators and others. From now on, the formerly shared intellectual privileges would stand withdrawn from common use without meeting the conditions imposed by the bodies where they are either patented or given copyrights. As of today richer countries are educationally advanced as well. Globalization both as a concept and practice intended to retain that monopoly. The G-eight countries can today decide about other non-G-eight countries. They have every power to dictate in other areas as well. The present day concept of globalization is but an extension of the same power configuration. Education is just one of the several areas that will get stifled by the few that have the power which unfortunately others do not have. And in this area India has much to worry about. With 3.5 crore remaining outside the schooling system we may have think of some other plan than Sarva Shiksha Abhiyan.

'Imagine There's no Country' by Dr. Surjit Bhalla is the title of a recently published book taken from John Lennon's song. The context is globalization. In the midst of all kinds of depressing debates about the impact of globalization on poorer countries his findings suggest that in the two decades from 1980 to 2000, the proportion of poor people in the world has fallen from 40% to 13%. In these two decades poorer countries have grown twice as fast as rich ones. The respective ratios are 3.1 per cent to 1.6 per cent. According to Dr. Bhalla one third of the global population resides in China and India. In the same two decades these two countries have witnessed record income growth. In a way, these figures persuade us to believe that globalization is not too bad after all. There are numerous other forms of globalization, just as there is a variety in the reactions to the hegemony of American power. If European Union has been formed to meet that kind of challenge, SAARC is the other alternative model. WTO and IPR are the byproducts of the same process. The eventual goal may remain full integration of all nations or may be total dissolution of the concept of division of people on any bases whatever but today we are nowhere near realizing this kind of goal.

I am not competent to discuss either the political or the economic impact of globalization. I could however go into its impact on Indian culture, languages and education. I share the commonly held view that an already fractured and divided society will get further subdivided and the technological revolution may sound the death knell to many languages, multiple cultures and create unbridgeable gaps between the 'digital have's' and the 'non-have's'.

The premise on which I am discussing the question of 'digital divide' is that we are well past that stage when we were being consulted whether or not we have any wish to join the bandwagon. Today there are no choices. Either join the mainstream or become extinct like dinosaurs or dodo. Having joined willy-nilly the rat race, as it were, there is no point in looking back. We are in the center-stage. We must take stock of what lies ahead of us and whether or not there is any possibility that we might still retrieve part of the lost ground. Each of these points has to be considered separately and contextually. We could react euphorically and say that a fraction of our population has done well both here and abroad. Hence, we are not likely to suffer too much as compared to X or Y. We may also stand up to say that the present scenario is too grim to describe therefore all that lies ahead of us is a grim reality and the chances are that we may do very poorly. I hold the view that neither of the two is a certainty provided we know what we want and are willing to act rationally and with good deal of determination and foresight. But first we should wake up to the impending reality.

The fact of the matter is that even in the USA the Government has come to realize that their society has been impacted very badly by the digital divide. In a paper written by Beverly P. Lynch titled "The Digital Divide or the Digital Connection: A U.S. Perspective" the multi-dimensionality of the concept has been framed by Pippa Norris into three distinct aspects:

1. Global divide – divergence of Internet access between industrialized and developing countries;

2. Social divide – gap between information rich and information poor in each nation; and,

3. Democratic divide- difference between those who do and those who do not use the new technologies to further political participation.

The above-cited paper emphasized the digital divide in its social aspects in the U.S. and paid particular attention to the role of the library in furthering equity of access to information. How much of this discussion will be valid for us in India could be imagined by the simple fact that majority of even urban population in India has only limited access to the Internet and few schools have libraries and the books and journals are equally dated or tattered, if they have any. For the sake of discussion only I am citing some figures from the most powerful and perhaps the richest country in the world.

In 1994, as the U.S. policy makers measured telephone penetration in the country since they realized that telecommunications policy would be influenced by the growing importance of computer and modem availability in households they created database. In 1995 the first Report, on "Falling Through the Net: A Survey of the "Have-Nots" in Rural and Urban America" was issued. Following its earlier formats of gathering data by household, the survey gathered household data on availability of computers and modems and analyzed data by income, race, age, educational attainment, and geographic region (rural, urban, central city). The report gave interesting data and provided benchmark data, against which subsequent studies have been compared showing the phenomenal growth in computing availability and Internet access between 1994-2001. In 1997 the telephone penetration was 94%. Computer penetration was 36.6% and PC growth by household was up 42.1% from 24.1% in 1994. The assumption was that PC penetration would be less than urban areas. In 2000 the PC penetration had climbed to 51.1. During 2002 the results show that currently two million new Internet users are added each month. Children and teenagers use computers more than others. In the lowest income groups too the growth was around 25% annually. The use of the Internet among the richest and the poorest was 77% and 35% respectively. Efforts are on to bridge the gap between those who have access to Internet and others who do not have such facility.

Compared with what obtains in the USA, now let us have figures given by Mumbai-based Strategic Foresight Group for India. The Times of India Dec.1, 2002, reported these figures. The report said," with different segments of the population and different regions of the country moving in various directions. India may formally remain united (note the word 'may'), but in every other respect, it will go to pieces within the lifetime of an Indian who has just stepped into adulthood. The report asserts that the disparities engendered by India's current development model have given rise to three broad kinds of economies. The Business class economy, which gives access to luxuries, constitutes a bare 2% of the population. The Business class is the one about which we talk the most. Then we have the Bike economy comprising 15% of the population—its consumption includes television, the telephone, the radio the motorbike and gas and water connections. The remaining 85% belong to the Bullock cart economy. While 50% of this class has access to the barest minimum consumer comfort, the rest however are just about surviving.

The figures in this regard appear to have slightly improved. With the coming in of the broadband and wireless telephony the above-cited figures are bound to undergo a sea-change.

Now to think of being able to compete with nations like China or any other country in Asia, the report has its serious doubts. The report would like us to have proper policies if the nation has to survive let alone compete and compete successfully, failing which we are likely to break up. The minimum we could expect from the Government is to reduce corruption and increase governing efficiency. An ORG-Marg survey reports that Indians pay Rs. 26,728 crores in bribe in a single year (Times of India Dec.18, 2002). In the year 2005 the data as reported in the Times of India (14th March) endorses the statement made by an Indian Prime Minister almost a decade back that the subsidized food-grain intended for the poor does not reach the target groups because of the immense corruption in the system. Surprising as it might appear, the teaching profession (something least expected) figures in one of the three top-most corrupt categories. This question needs to be addressed by the apex body of the teachers called the NCTE.

In a country like India governance is simply unknown and the rule of law is restricted to those that are poor and politically unconnected. If there is one country in the world where legislatures function overtime to make laws but no one is worried about their observance. The rich and mighty are as a rule above law and if one is also politically well connected then he / she commands more power than even the best paid executive from any walk in life. Now, this reality is not dependent on Information Technology or computers. The Indian lawmakers ceased to role models long back. In the year 2005 the situation is much worse than it ever was. The Indian lawmakers have outsmarted the underworld in more ways than one.

With more than a billion people India remains both a zoo – with tremendous variety of human existence and a museum where all historical periods continue to co-exist in chronological frames almost simultaneously. Few nations could boast of this singular achievement. When we can take pride in our cultural, religious and economic diversities and suffer social, regional (cow-belt and the non cow-belt areas), and geographical differences without demur what then is going to bother us? Under the circumstances, I think the idea of 'digital divide' is in reality no more than a mosquito bite or a minor irritant that will be taken care of in the process itself. However, if we are of the worrying type then we shall have to think of millions that are likely to die of hunger, unemployment and a whole lot of diseases without any medical aid. Depending on the type of category one belongs to 'the digital divide' will have its meaning and perception. By itself this term defines an idea and ideas have the unfortunate tendency of being interpreted according to the interest groups.

6

Modernity of Tradition in Indian Education

(The Revival of Indian Languages and Indigenous Systems of Education)

R.P. Singh

India has accepted the West as a model for modernization. In the process, Indians have ceased to be prejudiced against the use of English language, which during India's struggle for freedom symbolized foreign domination. Indeed, after independence, the mastery of this language has been instrumental in creating a class of rulers who are imposing Western ideas and institutions on the non-English knowing people. If this has led to a social division of Indian people, it is helping a few to attain a good deal of prosperity at the cost of others. More so now that the WTO regime is round the corner and the information technology has come to rule the roost. If things are changing on one front, on the other a class of people refuse to move out of the era in which they have locked themselves in. However, this state of affairs is still fluid; and the emergence of a new nation which may one day disown this language domination is quite possible.

In the context of India, 'modernization' has been defined by Raj Krishna according to whom it "refers to civilization and mainly implies a high level of literacy and urbanization with vertical and horizontal mobility, a high per capita income and sophisticated economy that has gone beyond the take off stage."[1] Against this definition Indian society has achieved only partly a degree of modernization. The West is a model of this achievement.[2] The fact that Indians are advancing in this direction can hardly be disputed. India has a literacy of around 65.25 per cent population and is gradually industrializing with the most advanced technology available in the world. Among the Third World countries, India is nearest to achieving the goals, which were set by her first Prime Minister who wanted to see India emerge as a technologically advanced nation and to this end he funded the public sector undertakings and created an infrastructure for future technology to grow. It is another matter altogether that today these public sector undertakings have become a source of nepotism and weakening of Indian economy. Even if India has lagged behind in certain respects it has the wherewithal of transforming the traditional society. On this score its past has been of tremendous help and the history of bringing in of 'new' knowledge and skills has been around for more than a century.

Raja Ram Mohan Roy was the first man to have fought and partially succeeded against the obscurantist forces as far back as 1833. There are signs that in the year 2007 a part of the modernization that persons like Ram Mohan Roy wanted may get reversed. A section of Indian society is condemning the government effort to introduce Sanskrit and make Astrology an optional course of study. One is not quite sure whether the contemporary stress on teaching values is a step forward or backward. The Hindu society, which constitutes the largest chunk of Indian population, has the resilience and a capacity to adjust to any shock whether cultural or economic. Therefore, as a society the Hindus are quite open and can accept any trend whether local or otherwise.

The Indians have therefore accepted that the only world language that can help in attaining any extent or degree of modernization is English. They bade good-bye to the old nationalistic slogans like 'back to villages' or 'adopt the village handicraft and attain freedom.' What has, therefore, happened after India attaining freedom is of tremendous importance to us in particular and to the world in general; Khadi is in but the old concept of Gandhiji to make the spinning wheel a symbol of self-reliance is gone. We want to go back to villages but the new strategy is to link the villages up with the urban centers and for that connect them with a network of roads, wireless telephony and the latest marketing techniques. That is how Panjab became prosperous and that is how several other states are likely to be in the same bandwagon.

In 1947 when India became free the zeal for protecting indigenous languages and culture was suddenly weakened. The bitterness shown by Indian political leadership against the British and their language—English lost its relevance. Not only were the days of Anglo-Oriental controversy buried in the dustbin of history, the contempt with which Macaulay viewed India's classical literature was also forgiven. India retained English as an Associate Language by an Act of Parliament in 1963 despite opposition from a small but highly vocal section. What Jawaharlal Nehru and others regarded as a 'window on the world' at one time slowly became 'the link language' in the country of its occupation and finally acquired the status of a passport "to governmental positions which control the economy."[3] Roman script was adopted in the Eastern part of the country for their tribal languages. The resultant mushrooming of English medium schools, 'rapidex courses' or 'English-in-one-month' craze, a sudden show of love for western pop music and faded jeans, extraordinary spread of 'elite' exclusive culture where besides deportment, western style of living has acquired a halo all its own and so on, are all indicators of the fact that the younger generation has disowned its past. Ever increasing international trade and a rash of new PR style is yet another dimension of India which goes to show her as a major exporter of finished goods putting a premium on strengthening ties with this world language. The new breed of doctors and engineers trained in the best institutions of the country are constantly on the look out for opportunities abroad. The latest to join these ranks are the information technology personnel and the success in this area has been so amazing that it has swept everyone off his feet. Once again the days of exporting indentured labor and unskilled workers are back but in a transformed form with the exodus of qualified, competent professionals abroad leading to a long, unending debate on the question of 'brain-drain'. The fire of patriotism, which had attracted the largest number of foreign-trained professionals back to India once to fight the biggest imperialist power in history, has now died out leaving no trace of bitterness against their erstwhile rulers.

Even the most heated debates on regional versus official language/languages have given place to other matters. The regional languages flourish as media of instruction to the highest level and their literary production receives national and regional recognition. The linguistic basis of carving out states has already been accepted so that no Sriramulu has to sacrifice his life for a non-issue.[4] The sporadic riots on languages issues which are no longer taken seriously and are regarded more basically an economic fights than any love for the language concerned are gradually becoming rare. The reason for all this is not because Hindi has been accepted as the lingua franca or because the superiority of one language over the other has been conceded but because jobs are available to only English-knowing scholars and the others find themselves at a loss when the question of all-India jobs comes up. The apparent sanity on the Indian scene about the language issue should, therefore, be ascribed largely to the recognition of an economic reality than to any degree of maturity, which Indians may have attained over a period of time.

The position of English in India has been considerably strengthened. There are several indicators of this phenomenon. Firstly, although all official documents are produced both in Hindi and English, very few prefer the Hindi version. Not only are telephone directories in Hindi not acceptable to the English knowing people, even those who are completely innocent of English would want to pass off as English knowing persons and therefore queue up for English directories. More books in English sell even as the editions of English dailies are multiplying in sizeable numbers. The takers of Hindi textbooks published by the National Book Trust and the National Council of Educational Research and Training are hard to find. The Children's Book Trust publishes more comic books in English than in Hindi. Secondly, writing of official notes in Hindi is rewarded and the Government of India shoulders the responsibility of teaching all its officials Hindi, but the result of all this is far from satisfactory. The fact is that Indian people are a pragmatic lot. They go in for what pays socially and economically.

Thirdly, India's dependence on a world language for its research, information and international contacts is too well known to be repeated. And one could go on adding to these pointers but they are all unnecessary now. More and more sponsored programmes in English produced in Great Britain, USA and Australia are being telecast everyday than was true a decade back and the demand seems to be inexhaustible. Indeed we have taken up the issue of foreign universities operating on the Indian soil seriously and a policy regarding them has as yet to evolve. If on the one hand we are accepting the world rating of our own institutions, on the other we prefer to send our children abroad for education so that the plum jobs fall into their laps at the cost of locally trained youth.

The best indicator of it all is the Government of India entering the field of opening Public Schools—once a preserve of the very rich. The Navodaya Vidyalayas are the new breed of Public Schools opened for the rural poor but brilliant children. Besides, hundreds of Central Schools have been opened which are regarded as the second best in the country. The reasons are galore why these schools are necessary, but the basic fact why they are rated the best is that they provide an excellent grounding in English and where Hindi is also taught. I have nothing to say about the intentions or otherwise or even with regard to the logic advanced in favor of their opening. For me the truth is that we have given seal of approval to the teaching of English everywhere and also accept the fact that this is the right path to advancement and economic freedom.

What we must note at this juncture are a few important facts about India's new class structures. Caste-ridden and regionally-biased though India may be, in order to describe a social reality we also must use the well-known term Lord C.P. Snow used six decades back to describe the British society. India has now two parallel societies with minimum communication possible. The English speaking/knowing urban elite knows nothing or very little about the majority of non-English knowing Indians. Thanks to oil boom the non-English knowing unskilled workers too hit the goldmine. They built big mansions in remote villages and are willing to invest in education for children. The classical example of this trend can be witnessed both in Kerala and Bihar. The results of this investment have not been universally beneficial. But, the urban elite have a vested interest in the preservation of the once discredited 'British heritage.' Therefore, they read, speak and think in English and attend the same clubs as their erstwhile rulers did. They have their exclusive schools, which charge heavy fees just 'to maintain standards.' Their children go to Mission Colleges and join All-India services or the multinationals. They marry within their class; and should the caste also match they then have the best of both the worlds.

The majority of the non-elites join government run/grants-in-aid/charity/ municipal schools. These schools may teach the same curriculum but teaching is carried on in Hindi or some regional language. And from then onwards starts the discriminatory process eventually leading these children to a future of becoming a second-grade citizenry.

The great urban-rural divide has become glaring in certain parts of the country. The villages have schools—a vast majority of them being single-teacher schools. The village school retains, by and large, their 'community centre character' where all varieties of social functions including political meetings and gram panchayat sessions are held. During summer and winter breaks its buildings serves as a barat ghar (wedding-hall) and when the teacher is away (which is fairly frequent as the 'absentee' teachers are a new political breed) the students indulge in free-for-all games. The seriousness with which the government issues fiats for running these schools is a veritable mockery where even the barest minimum facilities and climate for teaching are simply non-existent.

All Indian cities are facing an explosion in population, a large chunk of which consists of migrant, unskilled labor, adding a shanty township each month. Since they serve as vote-banks for the ruling party before every municipal or parliamentary election, they are regularized. The inhuman conditions in which these people live are seasonally improved and gradually municipal schools start appearing as pleasant surprises in an otherwise bleak surrounding. However, what is really surprising is that even villages are gradually becoming slums—where the landless laborer and the old cobbler or blacksmith finds it difficult to survive. With the arrival of technology in Indian farming and the formation of co-operatives in states like Maharashtra, Gujarat, etc. rural life has become a tad comfortable for the landowners even when their landholdings are not very large. With television covering most of the country's population and pocket radios available almost universally the complexion of social life is gradually getting urbanized even in remote corners of the country. While the banking services have now become available in majority of rural pockets, hoards of urban entrepreneurs have landed in rural areas in search of cheap labor and land for their industries.

The mushroom growth of plantation societies has more or less established that Indian can sense economic benefits from miles away. Once again the politician has helped in making these in-roads because backward regions of the country are being developed economically as part of their election time promises. The consequence of all this is that large, planned townships have come up in the most backward parts of the country equipped with schools, hospitals and other facilities. India's backwardness lives cheek by jowl with her biggest technological advancement. The newly constituted states like Jharkhand demonstrate the truth behind the logic. If the village school has no teaching facilities the nearby cousin institution has the best equipment that technology can create. The planned efforts, therefore, can have only a limited impact.

People allege that with the mass scale introduction of non-formal education, (a name now being given to this old scheme in its resurrected form with a new orientation is Sarva Shiksha Abhiyan) yet another class of the socially deprived is being brought into being. The non-formal education programmes have few takers and even fewer admirers. With the best efforts the Government of India is making to accord respectability to them, somehow people view this programme as an alternative to education and not an alternative to the formal system the latter, which in any case stands questioned. Even the fact that the illiterate must also become literate and help their younger ones to match with the others some day in future has not been told properly.

The survival in the complicated, technologically advanced age is not very easy and with no skills to eke out a living; it is getting to be extremely difficult to live with any degree of dignity. This sort of argument also holds no water because a section of Indian intellectuals have been taken by surprise by the Indian farmer who though illiterate has appreciated and applied advanced agriculture research findings to their best use. They therefore, say that technological advancement poses no threat to Indian masses, as they are quite capable of measuring up to its demands. However, illogical or hollow this stance may be, for the time being all do not reject it.

We may now take a look at the position of regional languages in schools and colleges and what steps have the State and Central governments taken to help improve this position. According to the Census in 1961, 1652 mother tongues were reported. M.G. Chaturvedi and his associate B.V. Mohale did a status survey of the language instruction in the country.[5] They argued that there exist variations in the reporting of mother tongues and 1652 cannot be accepted as a correct statement of fact. The schedule VIII of Indian Constitution accepts 16 languages as the major Indian languages but in reality there are 51 languages, which are spoken by more than one hundred thousand people each. There are 35 languages in which daily newspapers appear; the others out of the 51 have no scripts. All these 35 languages are accepted at the 22 brands of institutions being run by the government under its Education Ministry where nine subordinate offices help in the promotion of its language policy. In one way or the other these departments produce educational material in regional languages besides, at times, in English or Hindi too. These nine institutions are: The National Council of Educational Research and Training, New Delhi; Kendriya Vidyalay Sanghatan, New Delhi; Central Institute of Indian Languages, Mysore; Central Institute of Hindi, Agra; Central Institute of English and Foreign Languages, Hyderabad; Central Hindi Directorate, New Delhi; Rashtriya Sanskrit Sansthan, New Delhi; National Book Trust, New Delhi; and Commission for Scientific and Technical Terminology, New Delhi.

In support of its language policy, the Central government alone spends three crores and seventy four lakhs annually (1985 figures). This does not include establishment expenditure. Proposals are being made to set up an International Sanskrit University (there is a spate of Sanskrit Universities and now there is a Urdu University also) besides one for Hindi and a Board for the promotion of Sindhi. Most of these goals already stand achieved and newer ones are in the process of being evolved. The fact, that the Government of India is serious in its attempt should be obvious. Also, almost all major languages of the country receive support from their state governments. In brief, efforts are being made to develop all regional languages. However, the impact of this policy cannot be seen very concretely, nor can it be gauged accurately.

The third aspect of this problem is: What is being done in the schools to help retain tradition or modernize it? In order to answer this, we must, first of all know what our indigenous system is. The indigenous system of Adam's report died more than a hundred years ago, as it could not face its contemporary competitors. If indigenous system means the Basic Schools of the Gandhian variety, they were stillborn.

The Indian Constitution guaranteed to provide free and compulsory education to all children up to the age of 14 by the year 1960. Somehow, for this kind of education, mobilization of resources in men and material has not been possible until to date. Added to this is that Education has been made a Fundamental Right. The target of one hundred per cent literacy was fixed to be achieved by the end of 2005 (the reality is that it cannot be achieved even in 2015) by extending non-formal education/ serve Chickasha apian to all those who are not being covered by formal school system. A massive adult literacy programme has already been undertaken through its National Literacy Mission. In other words, India is determined to become a modern, liberal educated democracy within next five to ten years. To support this programme several schemes for industrial training, vocational education, etc., have also been put into operation. The efforts this time seem to match the goals.

The Eleventh Five- Year Plan has acknowledged the dependence of economic development on education. It is a big change from the earlier attitude when education was seen merely as an instrument of social change. Besides social change, education has a close nexus with development and modernization. This official confirmation of the obvious has significance for all.

The goals of education set by the Indian National Congress in their manifesto at the time of independence had emanated from the Gandhian philosophy of craft-centred basic education. In the course of last sixty and odd years, the ideas of Gandhiji have been thrown over-board and a new name has been given to craft-teaching viz SUPW (Socially Useful Productive Work) which really serves as a reminder to many that we had a Gandhian past. Beyond that, it means nothing to teachers or educational administrators.[6] However, computer education has been introduced across the nation and all schools are expected to offer it as a modern means of communication, knowledge and economic advancement. This is an indication that Indian education is trying to meet future demands on its own terms and as they say 'half-way down the road'.

In economic terms India is poised for a take off and its educational system has to offer a helping hand in this. In line with this, the Eleventh Five Year Plan extends necessary support to modernize Indian education. All kinds of discriminations on grounds of sex, caste or religion have been declared criminal offences already. Where else can we draw support for our thesis that Indian system of education is modernizing? It is, however, not trying to modernize the tradition, it is replacing wholesale the old traditions with new practices, which would with time become a part of Indian tradition.

References

1. Cited by Shah, A.B. and Rao, C.R.M. Tradition and Modernity in India. Bombay; Manaktalas, 1961, p.15.
2. Aiyar, S.P. Modernization of traditional society. Bombay: Macmillan, 1973, 275.
3. Pattanayak, D.P. Multilingualism and mother-tongue education. Delhi: Oxford University Press, 1981, p. xvii.
4. For the creation of Andhra State on the basis to Telugu Language, Potti Sriramulu immolated himself in fire. It set the ball rolling for the setting up to linguistic states in the mid-fifties.

5. Position of languages in school curriculum in India. New Delhi: NCERT, 1976.
6. For details, see Kurien, J. Elementary education in India, New Delhi: Vikas, 1984.

7

Role of Traditional Knowledge in a Knowledge Society

(Interpreting Insights for contemporary use)

R.P. Singh

(This paper seeks to examine the possibility of the use of traditional knowledge / insights developed over a period of time but lost in the haze of antiquity in contemporary societies).

"A technologist first builds a transport to travel on earth, second in the water and the third to fly in the sky. O person! Such technologists impart happiness, triumph and make us powerful. It connects or regulates such movements in the ocean with thoroughness. Likewise, they should train more people to multiply the number of more technologists." Rigveda, 2. 18.2.

Before we define *Knowledge* let us try to understand the use and meaning of the term 'traditional' first. Tradition lexically means "the handing down of opinions or practices to posterity unwritten" i.e. something society remembers to be useful and even after repeated trials finds the results consistently uniform. This is the scientificity of a tradition. All traditions have two components— the uncritical ritualistic, and the one 'open' for a dialogue before a change. All societies have to deal with both. The uncritical and the ritualistic form of a tradition, if followed make a society 'closed'. Invariably such societies get dominated by priesthood and become inimical for progress. It is the 'Open' societies that welcome criticism, dialogue, dissent and eventually progress. The best indicators of 'openness' are the multiplicity of educational managements and a variety in the school curricula. Such societies alone welcome criticism or questioning of a tradition and ignore the classes who oppose change or variations in social practices.

How does one define a 'Knowledge Society'? Firstly, let us try to understand the meaning of the term Knowledge. Knowledge is nothing more than rational, cumulative, classified, graded bits of information, which can be openly questioned. Information is a single point illumination of a query, which most of the time is an uncritical reply and whose source is invariably difficult to identify. A Knowledge Society is characterized by 'openness' and acceptance of new ideas and innovations. Being progress-oriented it is forever ready for a dialogue, experimentation and rationality. It is possible that some of us may hold the view that knowledge societies are a modern acknowledgement of a reality and that such societies have appeared only recently. This is not true. Such societies have existed in the past also and their quantum and the level of knowledge continue to surprise us. In fact in number of areas such as philosophy, ethics, science, literature, architecture etc the Greeks, the Egyptians, the Chinese and the Indians reached pinnacles of glory.

There are areas in which these ancients have yet to find their modern-day match. For instance, in Philosophy Bertrand Russell acknowledges that the entire development in this field could easily be summed up in a single footnote to Plato's *Republic.* The Pyramids continue to amaze us for the way they built vaults to preserve their dead and the material used to keep their remains unblemished. We have yet to find a match to Confucius or Lord Buddha and for the Aristotle's theory of the 'golden mean.' We have not succeeded to add a new plot to the seven identified by Aristotle or excel the use of Divine intervention in resolving a complex situation in a dramatic plot.

This means Knowledge exists in varying stages of development — some nascent, other developing or some fully developed. All traditional knowledge need not be developed afresh. In a way knowledge remains forever amenable to critical examination. Each sage of advancement has a context to consider. For instance, in the Indian context our society lives in varying stages of material and social development. A few of us have grown materially and intellectually so advanced that a comparison with European society appears legitimate. But the majority lives in conditions of extreme destitution and intellectual poverty. Generalizations therefore become irrelevant.

One must remember that societies are not homogenous. Just as it is impossible to find everybody to be identically healthy or sick, humans continue to offer a variety in existence. Similarly, there is no question of finding everyone equally accomplished or well-read. Therefore, all societies are identified in terms of groups of people who differ from each other either racially or culturally, and who have characteristics that help keep their identities distinctly definable.

Knowledge by itself is both multi-dimensional and unique. It has a typology of its own. Besides being eternal and contextually identifiable, knowledge has a variety and its set goals. For instance, human knowledge is different from that of the animals. Each Discipline as a Knowledge area has its own stock mostly different from that of the others ,and, even when the new stock is merely a derivative it seeks to explain the differences from remaining independent and un-submerged. Knowledge is distinguishable both by its age or the geography. When exported it changes its allegiance too and acquires a new identity such as Indian / American or Australian English. Knowledge could be static and / or developmental. The only thing that characterizes knowledge is that it changes its hue, control, definition and the state of development in terms of politics—whether religious or otherwise. Therefore, while knowledge in a democracy is always on the rise / development in an autocracy or dictatorship it can never be similar.

The Vedas are correctly regarded as repositories of all kinds of ancient knowledge and the acme of ancient Indian wisdom. In them lie the seeds (at times the finished products) of our modern knowledge. For instance, there is hardly any branch of knowledge viz. music, astronomy, physics, modern mathematics, yoga, alternate medicine, philosophical systems, literature, grammar and prosody etc. whose foundations cannot be traced to them. Few know that the binary system, which gave birth to computer sciences, has its origins in the Vedas. The yoga and the alternate medicine, which are the current rage in the West, can also be traced back to the Vedas. True, we have outgrown many of the Vedic discoveries and findings. But there are numerous areas of knowledge where we are still groping in the dark alongside the ancients. In some ways the contemporary astrophysics has brought us back to the Nasdiya Sukta to compare notes. Be that as it may, we share with them the desire to learn and discover.

We find the Vedas contain two types of knowledge—a) one that is eternal. This knowledge is given to us as a finished product; and, b) the other that changes with time and people. The knowledge they give us about the nature of humans—like health, moral or religious code, philosophy etc is liable to change either through deliberate efforts or Time. The reason is simple. Each age and Time defines its health, morality, and material requirements. But the constants like the need to work for a living, do business, undertake travel, evolve methods and modes of governance etc remain constant with plenty of scope for redefinition in their form and content. The Vedas offer us a variety of knowledge most of it being eternal/ or constant. They also lay foundation for a possible variety and scope for advancement.

Traditional knowledge has it own uses. The Vedas informed us way back in time that, "O people! You should discover the attributes and myths of wind and sun. they create water and juices of all types by penetrating through the clouds and make prosperity. The rain water does not stay with the sun. The origins of the water give knowledge about the sun and let us know that." Rig-Veda 2.30.2 It is perhaps since then the Indian farmers know the meaning of wind direction, the movement of the seven stars, the usefulness of the sun and moon, relationship of months with seasons and the interpretation of the color of the sky with prospective disturbances etc. They have been told over a period of time when certain birds appear, sing or squeak that portend a change in weather or when the black ants move from one place to another along with their household wares it signifies climate shift. For our purpose it is enough to understand that all these simple tit bits of knowledge passed on from generation to generation come in handy since they help supplement the predictability of scientific time-tested human awareness and information. If we wish to define the uses of traditional knowledge we shall have to conclude by saying that the entire stock of human knowledge is built up on the information handed down from one generation to another and eventually this amounts to measuring the level or extent of a society's progress. The ones who lag behind get classed as backward or 'developing' and are those who neither create new knowledge nor store the knowledge that is readily available in the form of traditions. Besides they do not possess in adequate measure the necessary wherewithal of transferring it either.

What we call scientific or objective reality is something that has a lineage of tradition. Repeated experiments or testing the reliability or validity of an information / hunch /or/ hypotheses makes the information thus gathered scientific— because it could be demonstrated anywhere to show consistency in the results. In a manner of speaking therefore 'traditions' in most cases are nothing but scientifically valid truths whose origins / sources have been forgotten or are just not readily available for comparison. This does not qualify for a sneering act on the part of those who generalize knowledge as a derivative of some available source other than mere oral tradition.

In the case of this country our traditional knowledge has withstood the test of time. The illiterate farmer is nearly as good a weather forecaster as a weather reporter who has the benefit of scientific gadgets. This comparison may not hold good always, but the predictability of both sources of information is seldom questionable.

The National Knowledge Commission (NKC) too has assigned a certain role to this traditional knowledge in their scheme of things. Although one may not agree with the definition of the traditional knowledge given by the Knowledge Commission (p.22) it is true that the 'appropriate application of this knowledge can enrich people's lives and livelihoods, provide alternative means of sustenance and generate substantial employment."

NKC has written that it is examining "the following aspects of traditional knowledge:-

1. The principles that should govern the documentation and use of Plant based drug formulations; traditional knowledge;

2. Traditional agricultural practices;

3. Culinary traditions

4. Traditional water-harvesting techniques

5. Traditional products, services and art forms not included above.

As it is the NKC has already received "a report on the traditional health sciences for their globalization". I suppose the reason why a Report on this area of traditional knowledge was the first to be submitted is because this branch of health sciences is more well-known and its practitioners have always been available ever since the times when Atharvaveda was compiled. But then there are other areas too that are equally well-known and nearly as much traditional— a few that have a direct bearing on our daily life and are linked with our food habits, naturopathy, environment, our rationality and mental health.

Though it is not possible to include all these areas in this paper or go into details of the benefits that may accrue if we were to learn the truths that were recorded in the Vedas but for the benefit of those who wish to learn about them I present only two or three aspects of that knowledge. We must remember that in this country a section of our population reveres the Vedas although they shall never read them or learn anything from them. Faced with the energy crisis the modern man should know that the Vedas had exhorted in their time the scholars to "know the nature and properties of energy and should take the optimum use of that knowledge." Rig-Veda 2; 9. 1 What is most intriguing about the Vedas is that they come all of a sudden not unlike a bolt from the blue without any precedence / continuity or knowledge of the state of society that produced them. We know practically nothing about the pre-Vedic people, the state of their material / literary development, their social organizations / customs or preferences etc. The usual support for any historical statement that one derives from subject areas such as archeology, written word etc. provide no help to an individual trying to piece together a picture of the time that preceded the Vedic age. In fact, a Marxist like S.A. Dange for instance has with the help of Engles tried to superimpose our contemporary logical analytical system on the times to which he doesn't appear to have had any clue.

I have tried to define a few terms used in the context of the Vedas. It may interest some to know that Sukta means what is pleasant to hear or something nice that has been said. In all, the Vedic Samhitas (as distinguished from the literature based on the Vedas such as the Brahmanas, Upanishads, Aranakyas etc.) consist of 20,500 mantras. The other thing worth noting is that a number of Rgvedic verses appear in the other Vedas too. The Vedic prose is rhythmic. The Vedas contain the earliest recorded poetry and prose literature of the human race. The Vedas are *no* sastras i.e. they are not systematized knowledge with a set of any scientific terminology. In most cases they summarize the insights gained over a period of time.

Samhitas means compilations. The Suktas and the mantras that are compiled under Rik are called Rik Samhita or the Rigveda. Similarly, the mantras compiled under Sam or Yajus are called Samveda or Yajurveda. The Atharvaveda is so called because Rishi Atharvan wrote a substantial part of it. For a long time the Atharvaveda was not regarded as part of the trayi tradition. Generally it is believed to be the last Veda because its content reflects a society very different from the society in the earlier Vedas. It seems by then the Aryans had come in contact with the local tribes and aborigines who believed in sorcery, magic and other satanic powers and all these impacts got reflected in the mantras of this particular Veda. In her book A Short History of the Vedic Literature, (Eastern Book Linkers, 1994, Delhi, (p.9, Hindi) Dr. Pushpa Gupta advances reasons for accepting the Atharvaveda as the last Veda. According to her (a) religion had peaked by then, (b) it deals essentially with the material world that deal with mundane occurrences of human existence, and (c) thereafter no new prayers were written.

I should like to explain the meaning of a few terms generally used while talking about the Vedic literature. For instance, the Sukta, means good poetry, or Mantra means speculation or summary of thought presented in quintessential form. The term Samhita means compilation. On the basis of the meaning and the nature of the content the Vedas are called veda-trayi. This use does not denote that the reference here is restricted to three Vedas only and the fourth Veda i.e. the Atharvaveda has been excluded. At the same time it is generally taken to mean that only the first three Vedas count and the fourth does not get similar weightage.

Though technically the word Veda means knowledge / gyan, the Indian tradition holds that the Vedas contain both the contents and purpose of the karmakaand i.e. the sacrificial rituals as well as the jnankaand i.e. the spiritual knowledge. On the basis of these twin purposes of the Vedas the sacrificial aspect of them is contained in the Brahmanas and the jnan / or the spiritual aspect of the knowledge is dealt with in the Upanishads. In fact, Apastamba titles both the mantras and the Brahmanas as the Vedas.

It is believed that internal evidence available in the sruti / or what was revealed or heard is indicative of the gradual complexity of language development that took place then. The ancients preserved the Vedas through oral tradition. It is common knowledge that to keep any language unchanged for a long time is simply impossible. A living language will invariably change both because of its natural tendency to absorb new words and idioms in its repertoire and to keep modifying pronunciations with each successive generation. This linguistic reason forced the ancients to devise a system that prevented such a change to occur. They therefore evolved a regular disciplinary system known as the vedangas i.e. the limbs of the Vedas. It was felt necessary to lay down general rules for pronunciation of words properly. Change in pronunciation leads to change in the interpretation and meaning of the words. This necessitated the formulation of shiksha and chhandas. The vedangas are six in number. They are: 1. Shiksha (orthography), 2. Chhanda (prosody), 3. Nighaṇtu (lexicon), 4. Jyotis (astronomy), 5. Vyakarana (grammar), and 6.The Kalpa (rituals). The ancients also divided knowledge into several areas of specializations. These knowledge areas are called the up (mini)-Vedas or the minor Vedas. These are: 1. the Ayurveda (the science of medicine and cure), 2. the Gandharva-veda (the system of aesthetics), and 3. the Dhanurveda stands for the system of defense sciences, and 4. the Arthaveda means economics or the science of wealth i.e. the production, distribution and utilization of wealth. For the development and growth of this kind of knowledge it is more than obvious that the ancients must have taken a very long time. In fact, the form in which the Vedas themselves have been made available to us makes an interesting reading.

I have taken up for discussion first that area which is currently of the greatest concern to the Mankind, namely— Environment. Let us see what the Vedas have to say about it.

Long before others came to realize the value of environment the ancient Indians had perhaps intuitively learnt that trouble comes from unknown sources and therefore it is better to take care of the immediate neighborhood first. This neighborhood is environment. By definition 'environment' means "The aggregate of circumstances surrounding organisms or group of organisms including the social and cultural conditions affecting the nature of individuals or community." Hence, the following prayer:

"May the five types of men, born to offer (the butter of) affection, and eager to perform the sacrifice, be pleased with my discharge of the function as an invoker; may *the earth preserve us from the troubles that come from heaven.*

"May you, spinning the thread of divine knowledge, follow the splendid light of the illuminator, and protect the pathways well...'

"The great river of life-conflicts flows alone, be alert; rise up, cross over, my friends; here let us leave those who are wretched and hence unhappy; may we cross over (this river) to secure auspicious boons." Rig-Veda X.54.5-7

The present write-up is addressed to those who have a very vague idea of how knowledgeable the ancient Vedic society was. In whatever form the Vedas have survived, they tell us enough about the Nature, Life and the concerns of the ancient Indian. Since I have for my write-up selected the Vedas as the principal area for exploration I have gone by the text that is available; therefore I have not bothered to include any analysis of the archaeological findings of Indus Valley Civilization to show how the urban populace of those times had evolved amazingly the most sophisticated and scientific urban water supply system and also the sewage systems that have been excavated.

The Vedic society is no less advanced and knowledgeable about the world around them. The Vedic Seers appear to have foreseen the catastrophe Man was likely to invite for his own destruction, therefore they had forewarned against indulging in such acts.

The appreciation for 'enlightened person' is remarkable for the ancients. Read what they have to say, "O men! I praise an enlightened person who shines and purifies like the fire kindled well with fuel, who is steadfast in non-violent sacrifices, pure, purifier, liberal donor, respected by many scholars, void of malice, wise with knowledge and humility and highly learned." Rig-Veda, 6.15.7

Experience informs us that mere knowledge is rarely enough to prevent trouble, and it is also true that we rarely listen to reason until the catastrophe takes over and we are left with nothing else but regret. In the modern high-tech world people have little time and even less patience to go deeper into any text even when it might have enormous value for one's guidance. Indeed, it is no longer considered necessary to read scriptures or may be it is even considered un-intellectual, if not infra dig, to try discovering any particular sense in reading them. Perhaps it is the job of a priest who is put paid for his services to read the same out in bits and pieces on ceremonial occasions.

Indian historians took considerable time to discover the meaning and the message that the Vedas carry and that too only when the Western scholars had started using the Vedas and their text for purposes other than those of mere scholarship. One must admit that it is the West that initially led the path back to our glorious past and furnished insight to find for us gems that had been lying hidden in the obscure homes of the neglected but venerable scholars.

I propose to cite here relevant hymns on each of the manifested contemporary environmental concerns from the text of the Vedas and show that the ancient Indians had the knowledge of the environmental problems but their future progenies, alas! did not have the 'Will' to act. The message is clear. If we failed once there is still time to mend our ways. This is the sole purpose of learning History. Historians as interpreters of facts are capable of delivering subtle messages to the posterity.

Although all the four Vedas were supposed to have appeared simultaneously the common belief is that the Rig-Veda came first. It is in this Veda that we see vayu or air being regarded as the soul of human beings. They realized the value of the air and talked of its curative powers. "Lord vayu is the soul and spirit of Indra and all other gods and living beings and is the seed of the world. Such a divine Lord flows according to its Will. We can only hear it but cannot see it. We bow before this lord Vayu." Rig-Veda X.168.4. Additionally they came to realize that air had its own curative powers. Therefore, they prayed," O Vayu! Bring your medicines and do away with all the ailments here because you are the only one who is full of curative powers." In the history of Indian philosophy there is discussion about the evolution of the concept of Atma or the source of life, which was at different point in time was variously identified with air, water, food etc. Even now we call soul as prana vayu. Since they rated all these 'elements' as divine and identified them with soul or life itself, it was unimaginable for them to have even thought of polluting any one of these.

Read, for instance, their feelings about Mother Nature:-

"I address this new laudatory hymn, with all sincerity of heart to the fire Divine, who loves it; and appreciates; may he hear our voice; may I be in the center of His heart.....like a loving well-attired wife meeting her husband.

"I address this new laudatory hymn, with all sincerity of heart to the fire Divine, the absorber of water, to whom the oblations of herbal juices (mixed with curds) are offered and in whom every living being like vigorous horses, bulls, milching cows and barren ones, sheep and goat are consigned to the cremating fire.

"The vast heaven, the spacious firmament, and the glorious unbounded earth; pay homage to the fire divine, Lord of the cosmic sacrifice; Nature's bounties such as lightening , the sun, the water, the wind and the cosmic intelligence, with potentialities purifies, recognize him with one accord.

"The rivers flow along with the dashing storms and sweep over the boundless earth, with them the circumambient lightening, spreading over a wide space thundering in the belly (of the firmament) bedews everything thing that lies within." Rig-Veda, X.92. 1-4

In terms of Western history the concern for environment dates back to 1962 (which is very recent) when Rachel Carson wrote *Silent Spring*. This book focused on the enormity of ecological damage brought about by industrial waste being dumped into the rivers. Then came the papers by Barbara Ward and Rene Dubois in 1972 "Only One Earth." Their project had been funded by UNDP. It brought to the fore the conflict between biosphere of Man's inheritance and the techno-sphere of His creation. Since then the voices of concern for the safe upkeep of this creation have not been silenced. The concern clearly is about keeping the environment livable. The express desire is for striking a balance between material prosperity and human sustenance. The 'Club of Rome' —funded by independent scientists, too has shown similar concerns and proposed almost identical schemes to sustain life on this planet

The 'Limits to Growth," brought out in1972, reported research findings based on a data collected at global scale on a mathematical model. The model predicted Doom and stated that continued resource shortages, crowding, pollution, famines etc will soon control current trends in population growth, natural resource exploitation and capital investment in agriculture. As expected this model was heavily criticized. Since then the problem remains where it was seen for the first time. As of today the problem is whether or not based on non-renewable resources is it possible to maintain a certain rate of sustained growth forever? We unfortunately are no longer ideologically neutral.

The Indian concern for the environment is as old as our civilization's origins. But did the ancients understand the meaning of the term 'environment'? Perhaps they did. But then what exactly do we mean by this term. "The environment (after all) is sum total of water, air and land, inter-relationships among themselves and also with the human beings, other living organisms and property." This definition appears in the Environment (Protection) Act, 1986

In modern terminology if one wanted to have a comprehensive knowledge of the subject the minimum requirement is to go through several stages of a variety of subject areas; such as Botany, Zoology, Micro-biology, Genetics, Geology, Bio-chemistry, Bio-technology, Oceanography, Atmospheric science, Statistics etc. It would appear as though we hold the view that if the ancients spoke on all these subjects with equal command like us then alone they would be considered knowledgeable enough for our good failing which, let us keep them under covers for a few recluses and the lonely.

Let us examine the Vedas on all these counts all the same.

For instance, see in this quote a desire that we have in common with the ancients, i.e. work so that one could meet one's physical needs and an airy house to live in. "I resort to agriculture and craft for removing poverty and ministering happiness to all. May I feel joy in domestic life! May our houses be sufficiently commodious, airy, fully comfortable, and built in the middle of an open space" Yajurveda, chapter 1.11

For an obvious reason an individual engaged in agriculture knows the value of timely and plentiful rain. In this sense we have not outgrown this basic requirement.

"Let us see with respect that earth, which loves the rains and is looked after by the clouds, in which is grown food grains like rice and barley, and where live all the four castes, and the other five types of people. Atharvaveda/12/1/42

As one reads the Vedas one is made to realize that the ancients suffered from the same weaknesses as we do, but they prayed to get rid of them through sustained efforts called the yagnas. For them," the yagna keeps away the thieves, refines and sweetens the speech, is productive of foodstuffs and is the bestower of knowledge and vigor." Yajurveda, ch.1.16

We see in the following few pages the type of knowledge they had of the Nature and its capacities. They desired that we do not transgress boundaries and remain within acceptable limits to avoid catastrophe. See here their knowledge about fire / heat.

"I describe the special features of Fire. It takes every type of matter forward. It softens iron ore etc. it burns everything. *It emits light. It beautifies. It is set up before everything else. It performs many functions and is used during many activities. It is an instrument for attracting attention, give and take and for food preparation.* ***Fire creates inside earth all varieties of gems and ores like gold, silver, iron, and diamonds.*** "Rigveda1/1

In the following quote the reader could see that they had knowledge of Vaastu and were fully acquainted with the powers of the Nature's Elements.

"O husband and wife! We want to construct a house for you; that is fully lighted by the strong rays of the Sun. For Sun is strong and capable of giving happiness yielding light". Rig-veda/1/155/6

About the Solar energy they say:

"Learn carefully about the presence of Vaishwanar Fire in us all. The same Agni/ Fire is located in all worlds and the same is working through Vaishwanar Sun doing all kinds of work such as producing light, growth of plants etc. Rig-Veda/ 1/ 98/1

Here is a hymn from Yajurveda (XXXIII.92), which talks of the functions of Sun: "Just as the Sun, set in Heaven, the benefactor of humanity, increasing in power on Earth, ripens medicines and grows food, removes darkness of night with his lusture, shines forth, so should ye dispel ignorance...".

"Just as lightning destroys insects that disturb sleep and spread disease, let us enjoy all the fruits and favors granted to us by the Sun and the wind and thereby let us feel safe against Nature gods." Rig-Veda/ 10/36/4

Or read their knowledge about the relationship of Sun with the formation of clouds and feeding rivers with plentiful water:

"O Gurudev! Just as strong, light -emitting Sun attracts the waters of these rivers toward itself and having done so distributes them through clouds all over again on the land, so do you attract students and instruct them with éclat". Rig 7/34/ 10

The Seers therefore enjoin us to learn to "Respect that special Guru who is powered by education, who is familiar with the work of Agni, Vaayu, Sun and other deities and knows all about the names, places and the births. You should respect those Gurus too who understand the speed of air and the lightening and who can tell you the exceptional ways to Salvation. "Rigveda/7/ 58/ 1

They offer a lesson or two in human psychology for compassion toward one and all.

"May that intellect which is inside me let that be full of feelings of welfare for others It is because of that the industrious, reflective and patient men work to gain both knowledge and the riches, and undertake to give charity, worship gods and work for mutual benefit, and that which is located in all living beings." Yajurveda/ 34/2

"Even as all spokes in a wheel are joined together in the center may my intellect also carry feelings of welfare for others because of the coming in of knowledge from the Rigveda, the proper methods of actions from the Yajurveda and of worship from the Samveda" Yajurveda 34/ 5

We could see their concern for the education of all, more particularly of girls. At least in this sense they were far ahead of us. While discussing methods of instruction, the Seers also talk of how to practice writing. Incidentally, the following lines throw light on a historically disputed domain. A few historians argue that the Vedic people had no script and therefore writing was unknown to them. I suppose it is possible to resolve that contentious issue whether or not the ancients knew how to write, what to write and the lack or otherwise of a script. The fact that they knew about the written word can be established even otherwise. For instance, on the demerits of gambling the

Rigveda (10/ 34 / 2) says that the faces of the dice **carried written** symbols. At another place, viz. Rig-veda10/62/7 there is a mention that the ears of the cows have **the number 8 written on them.**

Additionally, these lines also show that education of girls was common and prevalent. In their opinion female teachers are better teachers than their male counterparts.

"O girl students! Just as intelligent teachers introduce writing and reading of letters with the help of fingers, you should know lady teachers who know innumerable subjects and possess immeasurable learning. For your balanced development such an intelligent teacher will herself make all arrangements" Rig-veda/7/15/9

In case this is not enough to establish their knowledge about language / linguistics then see elsewhere they mention that mere reading is never enough because people learn at a pace which differs from individual to individual:

"A few do not understand the secret of **the language even after reading** it, a few others do not realize the reality even after listening to it but *there are others for whom the language presents her true form as does a beautiful bedecked bride reveals herself before her husband.*"Rigveda 10/ 71/4

"Language through its own symbols explains the wide expanse of knowledge and is able to illumine all intelligence fully. Therefore, one should put language to good use." Rig-veda1/3/13/

We see here the functions of language per se and its symbolic nature. It perhaps holds a lesson or two for the modern day linguists.

What did the Rigveda say about the nature of the universe (cosmology) / astrophysics that we live in? We may have advanced in varied ways but about the origin of the galaxies, stars and planets we are still nowhere being close to certainty. Even today we have not gone beyond the realm of conjectures in numerous academic areas such as astrophysics for instance; then how could we expect the ancients to be definitive about their knowledge, who definitely had no access to the present day scientific instruments, which make a Hawking so knowledgeable and relatively certain? According to the ancients the universe consisted of three regions— the earth (prithvi), heaven (dyauh), and the intermediate world or the antariksha. We are familiar with the term earth, but not with dyauh because this is one term which was employed to denote the vault of the sky, which is the place where the sun and the stars shine. They had an idea that there was an invisible world too where these stars and the sun retired after their daily ritual/ duty was over.

The Rigvedic hymns sporadically mention the abodes of padam of Agni, (1.72.2), Indra Pusan (1.162,2), Vishnu (1, 154,6) etc. In reality they appear to think that the universe consisted of four regions. The name of the fourth region is Satya Lok. Read Rg. (1.35.2), which says "Causing immortal and mortal to rest, God Savitr returned (to his abode) by way of the Satya Lok (i.e. invisible) world; he comes on the golden chariot observing the worlds." The Satya Lok was considered the abode of Brahma, the Creator. The later day developments have only added certain more Loks to the list. Only as a passing reference I mention here the seven loks that the Puranas talk about. From Bhu-lok upwards are Bhuvar Lok, Svar-Lok, Mahar Lok, Jan Lok, Tapo-Lok and the Satya Lok. Similarly, by that time the idea of seven 'nether' worlds had also grown and developed. They were called atal, sutal, vital, and patal etc. according to the depths at which different unwanted creatures supposedly lived.

Numerous references are made daily to the unusually wonderful understanding these Rishis had of the origin of the Creation, especially to the scientificity of their observations. For instance, the subject of Creation interested these Rishis immensely. The Rigveda talks of it in the Hymn 10/ 129/7 and Yajurveda in 10/ 129/ 3 etc. It does amaze one to imagine that even without the benefit of any of the modern equipments and gadgets they could be, at times, so precise in their observations. For instance, the Vedas hold the view that in the beginning there was nothing but darkness. It was the state of Nature, which could drown all without a trace. That extensive Nature, which is hidden in the Cause form, the same with the shinning glory of the divine God appears in the physical form as its effect. Compare this piece with the findings of modern astrophysics and take your own decision.

Read the **Nasdiya Sukta** and feel surprised at the latent modernity of reasoning and logic:

"What was the state during the Pralaya or total annihilation? Who is the Creator? What was the principal cause of Creation and what its principal instrument? During Pralaya there was no evil or good nor did the atoms fill the horizons? What was shrouded and by what? Who was the Protector? Did only the deep seas exist?

There was no death nor was there any life. Even the day and night had not taken birth. The lone Creator breathed without any life breath by his own will. Nothing superior existed beyond him.

In that dark existed, the un-manifested Nature like seamless water. Everything looked small before Him. Nature gradually manifested itself because of the austerities of the Supreme Being." **Rig-Veda** 10/ 129 i-v

A Desire was superimposed on what existed in the form of inner self during Pralaya. The seers could thus realize that the Good was latent in the Evil even as the light is in the dark. The creation could arise out of the un-manifested Nature. Slanted bright rays spread out of these three – God, Soul and the Nature. What was below was as amazing as the one who could serve as receptacles for that amazing semen above. If one went deep into the description of the origins of the Creation itself, we start dealing with the eternal questions of Philosophy whose definitive answers continue to elude us. Our understanding of the Reality is as remote today as it was when the ancients were trying to grapple with it.

In a hymn the seer says, "One thing that is beyond this world is matter, the material cause of this world, another thing even beyond this is the soul which is remote in rareness and not within reach of ordinary man." (Atharvaveda, Book V, XI. VI)

Interestingly, the Atharvaveda carries a section on the Vaastusastra—the art and science of architecture. Here a number of hymns talk of God being present **in a three-room school or the eight-room school**. One cannot imagine of a three rooms or eight rooms building without proper measurements and even building materials.

"Like the animal heat in the body and foetus in the womb I, the master of the house live in the houses, which are built with two wings, four wings, six wings, eight wings, and are constructed in appropriate measurement" Atharvaveda / 9/3/21

In fact, so great is the insistence on the proper measurement of the size of the rooms and the accurate mixture of mortar that one could seriously start thinking about the presence of the ubiquitous modern day contractor in that society too. One would be amazed to read about their express desire to make lighting arrangements that are necessary for a large room. The mention is of electricity and also of teaching aids. I must say I have failed to be specific because I do not know whether this light is not lightning and teaching aids something very elementary and highly primitive in character. These hymns in question are: Atharvaveda 9/ 3/1 and 9/3/11 and many more. The fact that God is present in all these classes of the school does suggest that schooling was carried on in built enclosures and not under the shade of the trees or in the hermitages only.

It is not quite correct that all gurus had equal competence. But in terms of their insistence on respect there is near unanimity. The impression that we have is that the Guru did not charge fees. May be he did not do so in the beginning. But no student could leave the residence of the teacher without paying the appropriate amount in terms of tuition fees/ guru-dakshina.

On pupil's return home the following hymn specifically desires that the teacher should make some relaxation in the strict rules that one followed.

"O the best Guru! The restrictions that you had imposed on us regarding food, sensuality and travel, please relax them now. O luminous with knowledge, Gurudev! We shall continue to observe all the pure vratas, and shall continue studying with unbroken regimen, the Vedas." Yajur. / 12/12

In fact, there is a mention that at the time of leaving the Ashram the student does say that he would like to know about the time one could leave the school and when does he invite the teacher home. **Atharvaveda (11/5/26)** describes how glorious the student looks on the completion of his education.

But here is one mantra wherein the teacher refuses to be admired by a student whom he regards to be a fool.

"O you, my pupil! Who shuns practice in learning, even if you are ready for employment immediately, **I do not like your praise because you cannot repeat properly even those lessons that have already been taught. You, who are famous amongst fools,** I do not like any praise from you. I would much prefer you becoming properly educated and earn reputation than what you are Right now. That would enhance my reputation." Rig-Veda/ 7/22/5

"The teachers who teach at the lower levels and offer expertise may they improve and grow. Those that teach at the middle and higher stages let them too progress and develop. The teachers of Som-knowledge let them too progress. Let all these teachers teach us the techniques and methods of prayer and the yagnas. Besides these teachers, those who know the techniques of the yagnas and are aware of *the way the Universe was created and are free from crookedness and have long lives may they too impart us instruction.*" Rig-Veda/ 10/15/1.

Let us now take an example of their concern for keeping rivers free from pollution:

"O God! Cast aside the vile man who pollutes rivers..." says the Yajurveda XXX, 8 and the hymn goes on to command, "Nishad's son, hankering after libidinous women; a degraded arrogant, friend of person harmful like a tiger; an uneducated person attached to low dancing and singing women; the demented, given to the application of magical rites; an untrustworthy person who befriends the serpents and fools, a non-gambler, who creates unnecessary excitement; a woman who creates split among the Pishachas, the thorny woman who favors the freebooters."

Look at the way they desire the trees to be protected," He, who rears the trees by erecting barriers round them...conduces to our happiness." Yajurveda XX.45

Read Yajurveda and see how in chapter XXII, hymns after hymns are talking of protecting oneself against the physical ailments and blesses those that help preserve environment. Hymn 5 in the chapter admires one who "protects beautiful objects like the Earth." The next hymn is even more explicit "Make the best use of fire. Take medicines. Derive joy for drinking water. Enjoy well the warmth and light of the Sun. Have knowledge of air and vital breaths. Perform yagna in fire."

They knew that "The Sun moves singly and alone. The moon is brought to life again. Fire is the remedy of cold. Earth is the vast field for production." Yajurveda Ch.XXIII. 46

To the questions:" What luster is like the Sun's light? What lake is equal to the sea? What is more specious than the Earth? What thing s beyond measure?" The reply is given in the next hymn. Yajurveda Ch.XXIII. 48 / "God is luster like the sun. Heaven is a flood to match the sea. Sun is vaster than the Earth. Beyond all measure is speech." It is difficult to find an answer better than this one from a Seer.

I now cite from Yajurveda ChapterXXIV wherein the Seers talk of birds and animals and their attributes and characteristics and where to locate them. The loving manner in which they talk of these birds and animals merely underlines the fact that they knew their beans about environment and wished to protect it. These hymns begin from number 11 and continue up to 40. There is not a single animal known to a veterinarian practitioner that is not described along with its typical characteristics. Read for instance, hymn 18 "The animals of peace-loving parents are smoke –colored and of brownish hue. The animals of parents who sit in assembly for propitiating yagnas are brown and smoky-looking." The next hymn commands" O men, bring into use the pre-mentioned agricultural animals" then comes the knowledge of the experts. "An expert in the knowledge of animals finds Kapinjalas in spring, sparrows in summer; partridges in the Rains; quails in Autumn, Kakras in Winter and Vikaras in the Dewy season." The rishis describe also the uses of each animal according to the class of people for whom they are intended. It is not possible to reproduce all the hymns to show the knowledge of the Seers or their desire to preserve all these species but it is perhaps enough if we appreciate their knowledge and perception from the following hymn (40): "Rhinoceros serves all warriors in preparing their shield; the black dog, the long-eared ass. The hyenas are used for protection against the demons; the boar is for the king who wants to tear asunder his enemies; the lion is swift like air; the chameleon, the Pippaka, the vultures are used are used for making arrows; the spotted antelope is used for preparing mrigshalas for the learned people."

The next chapter (XXV) opens with a hymn for protecting all objects worthy of desire. Read this hymn in totality," Learn for the teeth the act of biting; from the gums the method of protection; from tooth-sockets the way of pounding; sharpness from the fangs. Use the tongue tip for a learned utterance; learn the act of uprooting from the tongue; the use of palate by crying slowly; chew with both the jaws; drink water with the mouth. Acquire the knowledge of oozing semen from testicles. Recognize the Aadityas from the beard; know the path from the eyebrows; know the sun and earth from their motion; lightening from the pupils of the eyes. Observe celibacy for the protection of the semen; acquire knowledge through high character. *Objects worth acceptance are worthy of preservation.* Objects after one's desire should not be resisted. Don't show disrespect to your own men. Friends and relation should be fostered."

Whatever else may have been the motive of these Seers in commanding Man to worship God and perform yagnas, one thing is certain. They knew well their environment and wished to protect it.

What better could one offer in terms their understanding of the Nature's cycle around them than the following quote:

"When the clouds cultivate the earth with its waters; then winds are blown (for the rain to fall), lightening is struck, vegetation comes to life and grows, sky pours the raindrops and the earth then gets ready for the welfare of the world." Rig-Veda 5/83/4

We should remember that the ancients wrote an entire Veda on the science of medicine called the Atharva-veda. They went into details how a herb has to be identified and then they describe its properties for different ailments. They achieved and left behind knowledge of an almost fully developed medical science, which is currently proving to be helpful to the entire Mankind. Therefore they had prayed, "O God, create a man of iron determination for the implementation of a vow.....a forest guard for the protection of a forest.. and drive away a forest burner contemplating the destruction of jungles." Yajurveda, Ch. XXX. 19 one might as well put a question: "What else does a forest officer do other than protecting a forest and preserving wild animals and their habitat under his charge?" In the same chapter of the Yajur-Veda in hymn 10 the seer prays "O God create a physician for purifying our body with the eradication of disease; an astronomer for the advancement of knowledge; an inquisitive man full of cravings for knowledge; an extra-inquisitive man for desire of extra-knowledge; and a question-solver for establishing moral law." If read closely one can see the hymn telling us that all knowledge is located in curiosity and for extra knowledge one has to put in extra effort.

"O Spiritual juice (of wisdom and devotion) thou hast been prepared carefully for the soul. Let diseases stay afar together with the fiends of lust, anger, greed, pride and jealousy." Samaveda Hymn. 561 This hymn clearly states that "those who are double-tongued or crooked, cannot take delight of drinking thee." It would be clear to the reader that disease or physical ailment is as good as being crooked or a doublespeak. It is much better to avoid them both. It is only then that "those who are of calm nature like the rays of the moon, (will) be full of strength and wealth of wisdom."

I cite here a hymn (Samaveda, 1837) that has been interpreted differently by two scholars of eminence viz. Satvalekar and Griffiths, whose two versions are given below. Meanwhile the reader should also realize that it is quite common for the hymns being interpreted differently by different scholars. This is precisely what I wrote in the beginning about the difficulty of agreeing on the common meaning of a hymn or even of a single word. The Vedas can be read for different purposes, as they are capable of giving more messages than one can imagine. In fact, it is impossible to understand everything they say and why do they say what they actually say. Majority of the Indians regard them as **revealed** books because no human being could have been so wise as to cover all themes and subjects, besides all aspects of human life as they do. Probably for this reason alone that F. Max Muller wrote the following:

"What can be more tedious than the Veda, and yet, what can be more interesting, if once we know that it is the first word spoken by the Aryan man?

The Vedas have a two-fold interest for us.: They belong to the history of world and also to the history of India. As long as man continues to take interest in the history of his race, and as long as we collect in libraries and museums the relics of the former ages, the first place in that long row of books which contain the records of the Aryan branch of mankind, will belong forever to the Rigveda."

So much for the glory of the Vedas! This praise comes from a man who learned Sanskrit and translated the Vedas only to make Hindus Christians.

Be that as it may, the first interpretation is of Satvalekar:

1. "O Omnipresent Divine Mother! Thou art source of happiness. So endow us with strength and pleasure of great vision (realization) of truth."

2. Griffith's translation:- "Yea waters, ye bring health and bliss; so help ye bring health and bliss ye us to energy that we may look on great delight."

It is interesting to note that this hymn has something to do with water. In the next hymn the reason why water is mentioned here is made clear. Because water is known to be the source of life as it is one of the five elements or tatva that constitute life and at the same time water is also a cure for numerous diseases even if used singly.

The hymn number 1638 from Samaveda has two meanings. One is an external meaning and the other internal. The external meaning is as follows: "O water! Let your most prosperous juice be ministered to us in this world with the readiness that affectionate mothers apply to their infants."

The other interpretation is spiritual in character. "O Divine Mother! May thy most auspicious juice of bliss be ministered to us in this world with the readiness that affectionate mothers supply to their infants."

The next hymn talks of water being used for removing diseases. It is significant that the use of water as a medicine was known to them and therefore it becomes even more meaningful that this water has to be clean or pollution free. Look at it from an ordinary person's point of view by the time the Seers came to writing the Atharvaveda they had learnt through experimentations as well as through empirical evidence the curative value of the usages of both herbs and lotions including water. This Veda is a living testimony to the fact that science grows only empirically. And the seeds of modern laboratories were first grown in the Vedas. This is one History lesson that one should learn from reading the Vedas.

To end the write-up I cite the Rig-Veda X.1/ 46

"Lady of the Forest! Lady of the Forest!
Who seems to vanish from sight in the distance?
Why do you never come to the Village?
Surely you are not afraid of us.
When the grasshopper replies
To the lowing of the cattle,
As though to the sound of tinkling bells,
The lady of the Forest makes merry.
Sometime you catch a glimpse of her, and think it is cattle grazing
Or a house, far away
And at the evening you hear the Lady of the Forest
Like the distant sound of moving wagons.
Her voice is as the sound of man calling his cattle.
Or as the crash of a felled tree,
If you stay in the forest in the evening
You will hear her like a far voice of crying.
But the Lady of the Forest will not slay
Unless an enemy draws near
She eats the sweet wild fruits
And then she rests wherever she will

Now I have praised the Lady of the Forest
Who is perfumed with balm and fragrant?
Who is well-fed although she tills not?
The mother of all things of the wild!

And what greater respect could Man show towards all the elements of Mother Nature than the prayer from Yajurveda, 36/17 for peace or recite the Shanti mantra, which desires that 'let there be peace in the heaven, horizons—where the Earth and sky meet, peace in the vegetation, peace on earth, peace in everything' etc., and this prayer is always sung at the end of any holy anushthan or ceremony and this Shanti mantra may be accepted as the ultimate for any environmentalist.

I have already referred to the twin states of knowledge being both developed and developing. We have seen how the ancients were concerned about preserving the Nature as God's gift and now I cite a case of knowledge which has continued to grow ever since it was given birth. The current rage for adoption of the Yogic exercises, make us think that this knowledge is very recent origin. This is far from being true.

This knowledge was readily available in the Vedas. However, what has been added to that knowledge is something quite unique. For instance, there are today numerous schools of the Yoga (the hath yoga, rajyoga, karma yoga etc) and a few asanas may also have been evolved and even got patented during the course of development, but read what the Sam-Veda has to say on the subject. It is the seed knowledge which has thus prospered over a period of time.

"God who is realized through the practice of seven parts of Yoga consisting of Yamas, Niyamas, Asanas (proper postures), pranayama (control of breath), pratyahara (withholding from external affect) Dharana(concentration) and Dhyana (meditation) commands us in our own interest and is the constant giver of prosperity, riches and plenty." Samveda Book 2, chapter.2; 101

Until this day the Vedas have not been studied in terms of Knowledge they impart and their secular content has also not been classified in terms of knowledge areas / discipline. But if read carefully, the Vedas touch upon all areas of human interest; be it astrophysics, chemistry, mathematics, music, yoga, or philosophy, rules of governance, Parliamentary system, moral law, raising of army and its management etc. The Vedas have been preserved as collection of liturgies but the fact is that there are other ways to make their content examined and presented. Time has come when the secular content of the Vedas has to be classified, indexed and presented. In my paper I have tried to discuss this very role the Vedic knowledge can play. This should serve as an example for future / prospective researchers. The basic role of traditional knowledge is to offer ideas and suggest areas for further research. We must accept the fact that growth in knowledge is limitless comparable to the cosmos whose dimensions remain hidden from human ken.

SECTION - III

8

The Relevance of B.Ed Curriculum

Miss Nidhi Saxena

Teacher education in recent years has undergone metamorphic changes. The National policy of Education 1988 and Revised NPE 1992 and establishment of NCTE as a statutory body have influenced the plan and policies pertaining to teacher education program in India.

Simultaneously the major shifts in India's economic policies, liberalization, privatization and globalization have also brought about radical changes in the variety of teacher education institution. Social, economic and technological changes of the past decades are making teaching more crucial than ever. The information and knowledge society needs a continuous change in the role and the working of teachers. Being a teacher in the knowledge society, one has to deal with new knowledge and new ways for accessing knowledge. In the new technology era the role of teacher has changed and continues to change from being an instructor to a constructor, facilitator, coach and creator of learning situations. But the question arises, are we (teacher educators) really producing such competent teachers? Who can face the challenges of today's world? Is the curriculum of B.Ed. fulfilling the needs of upcoming teachers? If it has been improved or updated with the fast growing needs of market and society. No, certainly not so. How can we think of being a developed nation, where education is still in a developing phase and nobody is paying serious attention to that.

Curriculum plays a major role in shaping teacher's personality apart from methodology and evaluation system. But we mainly discuss syllabus when we talk about curriculum. Syllabus is just a small part of curriculum but curriculum in its broadest sense, includes the complete school environment including learner's experiences in or outside school. We should keep this thing in our mind when we frame curriculum of B.Ed.

Generally students choose teaching as a last option. They do B.Ed. due to some or other compulsion rather than choice but if we select students of right aptitude who really want to join this profession, by using right tool or test. Our labor of constructing curriculum will be fruitful.

The importance of teacher training is also reflected in the Supreme Court judgment. This is what the apex court said:

"Teachers should be subjected to rigorous training with rigid scrutiny of efficiency. This training needs to have greater relevance to the needs of the day. The ill trained or substandard teachers would be detrimental to our educational system if not a punishment to our children. The government and the university must, therefore, take care to see that inadequacy in the training of teachers is not compounded by any extraneous consideration."

In the new technology era the role of teacher has changed but the courses offered in the teacher education programs are of general nature and are not relevant for the professional development of the teachers. The curriculum should be flexible and address to the needs of the elementary, secondary and senior secondary level teachers separately.

In B.Ed curriculum too much emphasis is given on theoretical aspect. Out of 800 marks 600 marks are given for theory, only 200 marks for practical i.e. for practice teaching (Dr. B.R. Ambedkar University, Agra). Generally there are five compulsory and one or two optional theory papers in every university, which carry 600 marks (100 marks in each paper). I think, in every compulsory paper 75 percentage weightage should be given for theory and 25 percentage weightage for practical or project. For practical or projects preparation some of the units (which are already prescribed in the syllabus) can be used. When students will prepare projects or will involve in practical work, they will be able to implement the theoretical aspects into real life situation.

For example in the first paper of 'Philosophical and Sociological Foundations of Education' some topics can be utilized for giving project such as-

- Prepare a plan in your school routine (as a teacher) regarding value inculcation for primary students.

- Education as a tool of Economic Development (prepare a survey report of some slum area, people living below the poverty line, or some undeveloped nearby village)

- 'Social Change' and 'Agencies of Socialization' (In the present context).

These topics cannot be justified by teaching through lecture method in the premises of school campus. They can be understood in a better way by working on it.

In this paper 'Logic' should be included along with Indian and Western philosophies. If we want teachers to be skilled in rationality, logic should be introduced in this paper. The subject matter of logic should include the methods of judgment, types of propositions, hypothesis, definition, comparison, division, classification and fundamental laws of thought etc.

Logic is the science of reasoning or argument. Logic is concerned with both conclusive as well as partial evidence. The reasoning can be either deductive or inductive. So logic is the basic of all knowledge. The knowledge of logic will help the students in avoiding error and arriving at correct generalization in every field of knowledge.

In the paper of 'Indian Education and Its Problems' we deal with the history of Indian education as well as deal with other problems of education. History of Indian Education starts with Vedic and Buddhist period then comes the medieval period but modern period is too long. It starts from 1600 (at the time East India company came to India) and continues up to National Policy of Education 2002, which comprises a period of 402 years. In the syllabus generally no specification has been given regarding this period. Everything has been left on teacher's discretion. What I suggest is that some main topics should be mentioned (including various commissions, reports, and policy formulations). Student does so much hard work for preparing this unit but it does not carry much weightage. So it should be given enough weightage (at least two units). In their paper some current topics should be included like liberalization, privatization and globalization of higher education, NAAC (National Assessment and Accreditation Council), inclusion of educational services in GATS (General Agreement on Trade in Services), AIDS and Sex education.

In this paper some topics can be given for projects such as –

- Latest changes in the Educational Policy of your State (last five years).
- Environmental Education related programs in your city.
- Prepare a plan regarding AIDS awareness in your city.

In the paper of 'Educational Psychology and Measurement' some topics can be used for practical work during practical teaching. They should be taught to the students before going to practical teaching in their respective schools and right direction should be given.

- Action Research, Case Study.
- Achievement Test
- Diagnostic test & remedial measures.
- Intelligence and Performance test.
- Students can select topics for this practical work during practice teaching. For 'Action Research' project the pupil teachers may select any classroom problem, which they have faced during practical teaching and for Case Study' they may select any problematic student of their class. They will actually perform Achievement Test, Diagnostic test and remedial measures, Intelligence and Performance test and they will understand their relevance in the B.Ed curriculum.

In the paper of 'Educational Technology' working knowledge of computer with internet should be the compulsory part of the curriculum. Students should be familiarized with latest technology as in most of the public and convent schools teachers do lots of their day to day task with the help of computer. So B.Ed. students should be taught of maintaining cumulative record of students and preparing result card on computers. In this paper some latest topics can be included like e-learning (on line education) Edusat (Education satellite) video and Tele-Conferencing: ICT (Information and Communication Technology).

In teaching methods we should have 'work experience' related with the each subject. Such as in Hindi, English we can teach Hindi, English journalism. In Economics Banking, History-Tourism, Drawing-Fine arts (poster making), Home-science-Cooking, Science-Environmental studies etc.

Co-curricular activities and Sports activities should be the part of main curriculum rather than hidden curriculum. They should be treated as one of the subjects and should carry 100 marks, so students will take these subjects more seriously and will try to perform better.

In our country the concept of post-course internship has not yet gained currency. In this context of teacher preparation program, it should form an integral part not unlike many other professional programs. What I feel is that post course internship should be made compulsory and the duration may be fixed at least six months and if necessary it could be extended up to one year. During their internship they will be familiar with the complete routine or responsibilities of a teacher. They will learn maintaining attendance register, stock register, fee submission and maintaining receipts (fee record), organization of a variety of co-curricular activities like house system, school assembly, celebration of days, college magazines and journals, dramatic clubs, literary association, cultural festivals, games & sports.

The school experience program constitutes the most important component of a teacher preparation program.

Some optional subjects should also be introduced in B.Ed. curriculum such as Spiritual education, Disaster Management, Inclusive Education, General knowledge, Human rights education, classroom ecology etc.

We all know that progress of a country depends on quality of education, which ultimately depends upon the quality of its teacher. Good teachers are the outcome of good teacher education program. But the present program of B.Ed is more examination oriented and not oriented for professional preparation. The curriculum transacted in teacher education institutions fails to be translated in actual situations. It is time to wake up and pay serious attention to all this. We have to produce the best teachers in the world as it has always been our exclusive preserve.

References

1. Patankar, P.S, Padmini, M.S. (2005). Teacher Education for Inclusive Education, *University News*, Vol. 43, No. 18, 2005 pp. 124-132.
2. NCTE (1998). Curriculum framework for quality teacher education. New Delhi *NCTE*.
3. Swarup, Smriti. (2005), Fostering inclusion through Teacher Education: Innovative strategies and practices *University* News Vol. 43, No. 18 pp. 133-135.

9

Knowledge Society and its Teachers

Dr. Rajendra Mishra

Background: The quest for knowledge is a natural desire from time immemorial. Initially knowledge was acquired by limited means like signs and symbols, as well as through the locally available means in the form of clay, sand, wood, stone, etc. The first teacher on the earth is perhaps the mother. Mother after the birth teaches child how to drink milk to survive, how to giggle and also how to do other activities which in medical science are known as milestone of child development. You must be wondering why I am writing this as the background. The reason is that, the teacher is the first person who always desires to pass the knowledge to the learner through the best possible means and manners he or she has. This also led to various kinds of discoveries like slate, chalk, blackboard, chart, tables, compass, geometrical devices including today's computer, signboard, digital board, as well as things which are part of educational technology.

Initially knowledge was the privileged of a few. Later, it was made available to a large number of people from the population. Here one require a much better skills as well as means to impart knowledge to a relatively larger scale so that, the learners sitting even at the last corner is benefited from the same. Hence a method was devised in which, the subject expert / teacher writes about the areas of his specialization in a book form which was later on printed with the help of print technology in the form of a book. However, there was always a need for much better communication means therefore the advent of electronic technology for the purpose to spread the knowledge became very handy. Use of satellite for the purpose of communication was another milestone which changed the scenario in information and communication technology. With the use of satellite communication today one can reach any corner of the world sitting at one place and can deliver the message as per the requirement of the learner.

Use of electronic communication for the purpose of spread of knowledge as well as quality enhancement was done in India in the 19th and 20th Centuries. Today we have separate education channels for the purpose of delivering educational material, from the school level to higher education level. India is perhaps the only country in the world which has dedicated educational satellite- edusat for the purpose of imparting education and meeting the needs of students and teachers in various parts of the country. It is a well known fact that, in today's world if we are not empowered with the latest skills it will be difficult to compete in the national / international arena in terms of teaching and learning. Therefore, it is very essential that in the knowledge economy teachers' knowledge should be enhanced.

Development of Technology: With the use of satellite communication and especially terrestrial network through which the signals can reach to any corner without any glitch, India started telecast of educational programmes from the 80s onwards. Today we have school telecast of NCERT, higher education telecast of UGC-CEC, distance education telecast of IGNOU and technology education telecast of IITs. In this higher education telecast has 24 hour Higher Education Vyas Channel of UGC-CEC in which programmes/ lessons related to enrichment & syllabus based topics are being shown 6 hours a day with the repeat of the same lessons for 3 times to make it 24 hour higher education channel. Similarly Gyan Darshan Channel which is run by IGNOU also telecasts programmes related to school education, higher education, distance education and engineering related lessons with the help of various organizations, while IITs operate their separate channel to impart education through satellite to various parts of the country for engineering and IIT students.

The lessons recorded by the eminent teachers are being delivered through these channels via satellite through cable and satellite network which can be received in any part of the country as well as world wherever signals of such network is available. However, this technology was still having the limitation of one way communication. The interactivity in this mode was firstly not possible and secondly if possible it was very expensive. The concept of educational satellite launched in India has made the educational communication more effective and facilitates the transmission of these programmes through the internet. I am not going into the details of development of internet based gateways reason being this is mostly available on various other material. I would like to leave this and suggest the learners and the readers of this research paper to please go to internet and search through the search engines regarding the development of this kind of technology to get the history aspect.

The First Internet Based Communication: The internet based communication started for the purpose of transfer of educational data by 2 students in the University of California, Los Angels. They linked 2 large computers using a 15 feet cable and tested a new way to exchange data on September 2, 1969.[1]

Educational development of internet format as well as multi channel communication through satellite significantly influenced the educational communication.[2]

With this brief document I want to emphasize that today it is possible to deliver knowledge through various means which includes print, electronic transformation, satellite communication including internet based transmission. In the coming parts I am going to discuss about how technology can be used to enhance the skills of the teachers through which they become more empowered to deliver knowledge to the learners more effectively keeping in mind the present scenario in which India is poised to become knowledge economy and also knowledge driven society. In India EDUSAT is one big step to utilize the best of the technological option to make teaching learning more interesting. One needs to know that if you as a teacher do not enjoy the teaching then how you expect the learner to have joy in learning.

Knowledge Society: It is essential to understand that to make India a very vibrant knowledge society we need to develop methodologies and infrastructure to train manpower which in turn will deliver the knowledge resources for the future generations. For this purpose, proper use of educational technology, skill orientation and enhancement of the quality of the teachers' knowledge becomes most pivotal. In this context I would like to mention that we need to revamp the teachers training curriculum in which information communication technologies should become a major part in the development of the lessons along with the following aspects:

(1) Instructional design for the purpose of training teachers especially for higher education purpose (teachers teach in colleges and universities needs to be told about the instructional design especially who they have never trained in education as a subject where they are taught these areas).

(2) Technology upgradation.

(3) Infrastructure to develop use of multimedia and other such facilities.

(4) Requirement of the trainers to impart such trainings to the teachers with skill up gradation.

It is essential to understand that skill upgradation of teacher is the only way through which we can impart the knowledge more effectively. This also will help us in developing the knowledge wares more effective and more interesting from the point of view of learners. For this purpose we need to train all our teachers with the latest educational technology material as well as with all other inputs which includes development of presentations through PPTs with the use of multimedia, graphics, charts as well as if possible videos to show live demonstration.

It is worthwhile to mention that today with the constitution of Knowledge Commission by the Government of India the emphasis is more towards the requirement to face current and future challenges. India can only become knowledge economy if it starts enrolling more than double the number of students in higher education. Presently we have only 9.5% of the total population which is going for higher education. As per the Knowledge Commission's recommendations we need to enroll minimum 15% learners in the next 5 years to make India a vibrant knowledge economy. For this purpose it is very essential that we should also develop skilled manpower as well as infrastructure in which we are able to sustain the pressure of training and skill upgradation. India do not have the required standards for the purpose of quality enhancement in various areas of skill up gradation whether it is school level, higher education level, technology level. We need to develop manuals in which we can emphasize the need of such quality inputs.

Quality: No country or no nation cannot become self-sufficient and cannot take the fruits of development if it is not quality conscious. To make India knowledge economy as well as super power by 2020 as per our vision and mission we need to educate masses, develop quality standards to impart the knowledge to learners and to general masses who are interested in developing their skills. For this purpose training in high quality standards will be very essential.

Teachers of today although are very well placed to get the benefits of latest technologies, they are either deprived of the facilities or lack of motivation hence they are unable to impart the kind of education that they need to do today. CEC has conducted 10 training programmes in the area of skill development for development of E-content material and multimedia and has found that out of the 700 teachers it has trained, so far none of them have said that they are knowing all these skills or they do not have interest knowing these skills. Rather all of them have said overwhelmingly that the training for development of E-content has opened their vistas and has also helped them in developing their lectures in a much better way. In one of the training programmes the teachers told me that in the entire 35 years of their career, for the first time they realized that how teaching can become more interesting and joyful. provided you use the simple and the latest methods by which you can impart the knowledge through the means of instructional design methodology.

To conclude I would like to mention that the teachers of knowledge society are faced with 2 kinds of dilemmas. One is availability of infrastructure and second is opportunity to get their skills upgraded. In organizations like CEC and such other places, facilities do exists. However these facilities can cater only to a very limited number of people. Hence with the help of latest technology it is possible to replicate these training programmes and upgrade the skills of the teachers by way of imparting training at the places where such facilities can be created with the help of Academic Staff Colleges, B.Ed Colleges and so on. At the end I would like to mention that the days are going to come when you if as a teacher are not willing to upgrade and update oneself, then you will have no place in the teaching fraternity. India can only become knowledge society as well as knowledge economy, provided it has got quality conscious citizens, students, teachers as well as the willingness to address the needs of the present situation to create a more vibrant and knowledgeable generation for the future development of mankind.

Suggested Readings

1. Sharma G.D. – Knowledge Packaging for face to face and self based learning; Development of e-content on higher education – reading material and CD resources – 2005, CEC, N.D.
2. Skinner, Thorndike, Watson. # Online available – http://user.www.sfsu.edu/~rsauzier/thorndike.html
3. Tim O'Shea and Eileen Scanlon, Virtual Learning Environments and the Role of the Teacher: Report of a UNESCO/Open University International Colloquium, pp.14-16, Paris/Milton

Keynes, United Kingdom, UNESCO/Open University Institute of Educational Technology, 1997. (Mimeo).

4. Pawan Agarwal – Higher Education – From Kothari Commission to Pitroda Commission; Economic and Political Weekly – February 17, 2007.
5. M. Anandakrishnan – Critique of Knowledge Commission – Economic and Political Weekly – February 17, 2007.
6. R Mishra - EDUSAT in teacher training and education; Anweshika –Indian journal of Education, June, 2006.

10

Teacher Education and NCTE: Fencing eats the Crops

Dr. C.P. S. Chauhan

It is rightly said that 'there can be marvelous teaching in muddy walls and muddy teaching in marble halls'. What it means is that a school does not mean simply a magnificent building with beautiful gardens and lawns, rich laboratories and libraries, and a large playground; rather, it means a 'learning environment' created by visionary and imaginative teachers. Education Commission (1964-66), in its report, emphasized the importance of the quality, competence, and character of teachers and their professional preparation for qualitative improvement of education. "Investment in teacher education can yield very rich dividends because the financial resources required are small when measured against the resulting improvements in the education of millions. The essence of a teacher education program is its 'quality' without which, it becomes, not only a financial waste, but also a source of overall deterioration in educational standards", the Commission added. When India became free in 1947, it was expected that the post- independence era would witness revolutionary changes in the basic structure of education. But, unfortunately the colonial system was allowed to continue and it still continues. Within education, teacher education has been most neglected till now. As education system in our country expanded after independence, the need of more and better teachers increased.

Quantitatively, the teaching profession is the largest among all the professions of equivalent status with about 6 million members—5.5 million working at school stage and 0.5 million at higher education stage. In spite of the fact that teaching is not a preferred vocation for most of our graduates, teachers constitute a major portion of our workforce. As evident from the share of funds allocated in the plan and non-plan budgets, 'education' is not a significant sector of economy for our government. On the other hand, general public is also not satisfied with our education system, especially, the performance of teachers. There is a general complaint that teachers at all levels either 'do not reach' or 'cannot teach'. The reasons for 'do not teach' may be related to their social and moral aspects of behavior while those for 'cannot teach' may be traced in the process of their academic and professional preparation.

The National Policy on Education-1986 laid greater stress on quality of teacher education than ever before and proposed that the National Council for Teacher Education (NCTE) should be given a statutory status. The proposal was approved by the government through an Act of Parliament in 1993. The statutory NCTE was created 'to achieve planned and coordinated development of teacher education system throughout the country and to ensure the maintenance of norms and standards in teacher education system', and also 'to stop its commercialization'. The organization started functioning in August 1995. The first major task which NCTE undertook after its inception was to ask the existing teacher education institutions to seek from it a formal recognition of their courses. For this purpose inspections were conducted by the NCTE which accounted for huge expenditure from public funds. The process of inspection followed by formal recognition of old institutions continued for at least five years. It was difficult to understand why an institution functioning for over a hundred years should seek formal recognition from the NCTE after awarding thousands of (unrecognized?) degrees and diplomas. It is difficult to justify the expenditure, which ran into millions of rupees, on this exercise. It would have been more reasonable had this process been adopted only for creating new and quality teacher training institutions.

With the inception of NCTE as a quality control mechanism, it was expected that teacher education system in India would underga a radical change. But unfortunately, the new teacher education 'curriculum framework' developed and published by it in 1998 also followed the traditional lines. It included traditional theory courses and practice teaching to be conducted by the traditional methods. The only significant and noticeable changes, as proposed by then experts of the NCTE, were the ones regarding extension of the duration of training courses from one year to two years and revival of the four-year integrated teacher education programs. It appeared that the thought processes underlying the formulation of the new curriculum framework were least influenced by the new developments in information and communication technology. The ICT has revolutionized the teaching learning process at all levels and in all fields, but teacher education has not seen the light of the day, courtesy the 'traditional outlook' of then NCTE officials and experts. Unfortunately, our experts and policy planners go by folklore without carrying out field surveys themselves or taking any clues from available research literature. The NCTE never thought of analyzing the teachers' job to identify the desired teaching behaviors and competencies and develop curriculum accordingly. Such an effort would have been a genuine gesture of sympathy to the poor taxpayers who finance such huge projects.

The single publicly visible achievement of the NCTE is that it has multiplied the number of teacher education institutions through a process of development of norms, conduct of inspections, and award of recognition to all those institutions which could somehow make the inspection teams submit favorable reports to the concerned regional committees. This process involved rampant corruption. When an element of corruption crept into the process of inspection many senior teacher educators either withdrew voluntarily or deliberately excluded from the panels because they were 'inconvenient and non-cooperative'. Gradually, the 'envelop culture' of underhand dealings took strong roots and selected people who were ready to rub their palms with the NCTE functionaries for sharing the grease, became professional inspectors. Now, the stage has reached that teachers of small degree colleges with a few years of experience are repeatedly sent by the NCTE for conducting inspections because they are 'convenient and cooperative'. A clan of politicians and businessmen as 'B. Ed. mafia' has developed over the years which dominates the decision making process through their political links. The structure of regional committees of the NCTE provides a live evidence of this fact. Sometimes, members of the inspection team do not even formally visit the institution and write the inspection report inside the air-conditioned lobbies of the starred hotels hired in advance by the hosts to ensure their comfortable stay. One interesting thing is that proposals of owners of private institutions are processed very expeditiously while those of central universities gather dust for years. This is simply because central universities can not do what private people can. One who is interested to know more about the functioning of this organization is advised to read the report of the Anand Sarup Committee which was appointed to inquire into the affairs of some teacher education institutions in Bihar and West Bengal under Eastern Regional Committee. The opening sentence of the report reads as follows: "This is a narrative about the so-called Fake Institutions for Teacher Education, which reportedly came up in Bihar following the establishment of NCTE in 1995, after the NCTE Act came into force on the17th of August 1995." What happened to this report is not known. Maybe, as usual, it has gone to a waste-paper basket.

The net result is that secondary teacher education institutions have gone up from only a little more than 600 in 1994 to more than 3000 (most of them having substandard quality) within a short period of one decade. Nobody, including the NCTE officials, seems to be concerned about the quality of training imparted in these institutions. It appears that saving their chairs/positions is the topmost item on their agenda. Taking full advantage of the situation, the clever businessmen abandoned their traditional dealings in onions and potatoes and started B. Ed. colleges in the go downs thus vacated, because they saw in it huge monetary returns for meager investment. The designation of principal has been renamed as 'director' by private managements where most of the, so-called, directors are superannuated who could rise not higher than the position of a lecturer in their regular job. Has the NCTE approved such designations? Instances have been reported where a single qualified person is shown working as lecturer in several B. Ed. colleges while, in fact, he works nowhere and draws partial salary from all of them. The persons with B. Ed. degrees are teaching B. Ed. students on meager salaries. The general feeling among teacher educators is that the quality of teacher education was better before the inception of the NCTE. Of course, some pseudo-educationists made hay at the sun-shine during the formative years of NCTE. It was like an old-age home for them. They traveled by air even for short distances of 250 kilometers at the cost of poor people of the country. If air bills of a few persons associated with the NCTE those days are re-examined, startling facts will come to light.

Unfortunately, teaching is not recognized as a profession by our government at par with professions like engineering, medicine and law. No non-medico can be posted as Chairman of Medical Council of India. But, in the case of teacher education this principle is not followed. The government just picks up anybody irrespective of his seniority and caliber and places him on the highest position in the field of teacher education. That is why all chairpersons of the NCTE appointed by the government so far have been persons without any formal training/degree in teacher education. The genuine teacher educators have been content with only the second position. But, they have had hard times because their bosses had stronger political connections. It is really interesting to see that training is essential even for a primary school teacher, but a person who controls the entire teacher education system of the country does not require any kind of formal training. If a person can become 'the best teacher educator of the country' without formal training, then existence of such a large system of teacher education is not justified. If one has a casual glance over the list of members of various Regional Committees constitutes by the NCTE, one finds that these committees are full of those who have nothing to do with education and teaching, not to talk of formal training as teachers. This tells the underlying story and gives the message that teacher education is not recognized by the government as a specialized professional training.

Institutions are created with great fanfare, but while manning them, they are hit at the very roots. The body, as a quality control mechanism, was created to fulfill the twin objectives of achieving planned and coordinated development of teacher education and stopping its commercialization. Unfortunately, since the inception of NCTE the quality of teacher education in India has gone down and its commercialization has risen to its peak. The results are contrary to the intensions. The fundamental problem is that NCTE never recognized its regulatory functions which were assigned to it by the Act of Parliament in 1993. There has been a mismatch between the vision and the ground reality. It passed most of its time in writing curriculum frameworks and books on educationists which should have been a secondary business, the primary being making efforts for determination and maintenance quality. Now, it is high time for the government to think whether the existence of NCTE or any such organization is worth the expenditure involved in its maintenance. We already have the NAAC which is also a regulating body for higher education institutions including those of teacher education, then why do we need another organization for the same purpose? Let us not forget that poor people pay for these projects.

11

N.C.T.E. –Its Paradoxes and Contradictions

Dr. Jitendra Sharma

When in 1995 the National Council for Teacher Education (N.C.T.E.) came into being as a consequence of the National Council for Teacher Education Act, 1993 the persons like me had jumped on their feet and had celebrated the occasion as a milestone thinking that the teacher education in India would join the company of the elite professional courses like that of Medical and Engineering, etc. The arrival of the N.C.T.E. on the scene was also considered a positive event by the teacher-educators of Rajasthan, the State I come from, since Rajasthan was a peculiar State wherein Universities' affiliated Teachers' College under the Secondary School set up. It was and is a bizarre situation where the teachers of these Colleges are not required to possess the UGC stipulated qualifications nor are they paid the UGC pay-scales and salaries. which their counterparts in Universities and academic colleges get within and outside Rajasthan.

Now, when the talks of repealing of the NCTE Act 1993 and thus winding up of the NCTE are in the air, and the AIU Newsletter in its issue of August 13-19, 2007 (Vol. 45, No. 33) carried three Papers on the functioning and working of the NCTE, I was also prompted to chip in.

Though the role and functioning of the NCTE since its establishment have not always been in the focus of those working in the area of the teacher education, a curious attitude towards it has been visible since the day the news appeared in the media about Sudip Banerjee Committee's recommendation for the repeal of the NCTE Act. A few voices have been heard against such a move but looking to the enormous number of the teacher education institutions in the Country this voice-raising by a handful of the educationists is just a reflection of all-pervasive sense of alienation / disenchantment with, or an almost total no-concern for NCTE of the teacher educators working across the Country. For them, it appears as if, the existence or otherwise of the NCTE is inconsequential. Had the NCTE been the real life-line of the teacher education in the country the reaction would have been very different.

Such a total apathy towards the NCTE is not without reasons. In fact, the NCTE during the twelve years of its existence has never let anybody feel that it is a "statutory" and "regulatory" body in the real sense of the terms. Its working has been found to be so wayward and lopsided that while on almost all occasions it could get its statutory and regulatory status vindicated by the Supreme Court and/or the High Courts, on most other occasions it maintained a very enigmatic and mysterious silence even when the reports of the blatant violations of its Norms and Standards for different Teacher Education programs were made to the Headquarters as well as to the Regional Offices. Its Janus-like approach has perhaps been one of the many causes for the disillusionment in the teacher education fraternity towards the NCTE.

At the very outset allow me to insist that it must be borne in mind that the NCTE is a regulatory and statutory body. These two words – "regulatory" and "statutory" – are very significant and must never be lost sight of while assessing the roles and functions of the NCTE.

Besides, it would be befitting here to first of all consider the constitutional provisions pertaining to the division of powers in the area of running the different layers of formal education in the Country. It is necessary too to dispel some very serious doubts about the roles of the Central Government vis-à-vis the State Governments. Nothing in this regard would be more appropriate than to quote the following from the Order passed by the Hon'ble High Court of Madras on 23.2.2005 (in the writ appeals in 4204 of 2004 and writ appeal nos. 4205, 4237, 4240, 4241 of 2004 and 104, 1050, 180, 305, 306 and 307 of 2005 and W.A.M.P. Nos. 7969, 7970, 8026, 8029 to 8031/2004, 150/2005, 235/2005, 299/2005, and 553 to 557/2005):

Para18. "Now we shall consider the power to legislate on the subject of education. Previously the said power was provided in Entry 11 of List II of Schedule VII of Constitution of India. By virtue of 42nd Amendment of the Constitution which was given effect to from 3-1-1977, the subject of education has been classified as follows:

"Union list - list I - Entry 66

Co-ordination and determination of standards in institutions for higher education or Research and Scientific and technical institutions.

Concurrent list - list III - Entry 25

Education including technical education, medical education and Universities, subject to the provisions of Entries 63, 64, 65, and 66 of list 1; Vocational and technical training of labor."

From the above said re-classification of the legislative source of power on the subject of education, it is seen that the Union of India is competent to enact laws relating to higher education, technical institutions etc. The Supreme Court of India in interpreting the said Entries, has categorically held that there can be no State enactment repugnant to the law enacted by the Parliament and that the provisions contained in any of the State enactment such as Tamil Nadu Private Colleges Act, Madras University Act etc., which are inconsistent with the provisions contained in any of the Central Acts such as AICTE Act, MCI Act, Dentist Act etc., are ultra vires to that extent of repugnancy. Useful reliance was also placed on the same judgments in Adhiyaman college case; Thirumuruga Kirupananda Variar's case; and Jaya Gokul's case which are in the following effect:-

(1) 1995 (4) SCC 104. In this decision it has been categorically held that neither the State Government nor the University have got power to enact law on the subject falls under Entry 66 of List I and that the existing law to the extent of inconsistent with the provisions made in the AICTE Act is ultra vires and unenforceable.

(2) 1996 (3) SCC 15. In this decision the Supreme Court has held that prior permission of State Government to start a new Medical College is invalid on the ground of repugnancy. It is further held that Section 5 (5) of the Medical University Act enacted by the State Act is held as repugnant to Section 10-A of Indian Medical Council Act.

(3) 2000 (5) SCC 231. By re-capsulating the dictum laid down in Adhiyaman's case, the Supreme Court specifically ruled that the University cannot impose conditions for affiliation in contravention of the provisions contained in the Central Act viz., AICTE Act. Thus, the position of law and the validity of existing law of the State Enactments have been made crystal clear in the above stated judgments of the Supreme Court.

Para19. The Teacher Training Institution (B.Ed., course) is referable to Entry 66 of List I and as such the Parliament promulgated the NCTE Act 1993 which came into force with effect from 1-7-1995. The NCTE framed Regulations 2002 in exercise of power under Sections 14, 15 and 32 of NCTE Act. In this regard, it is also relevant to note the preamble of the NCTE Act which runs as follows:

"An Act to provide for the establishment of a National Council for Teacher Education with a view to achieving planned and coordinated development of the teacher education system throughout the country, the regulation and proper maintenance of norms and standards in the teacher education system and for matter connected therewith."

In a relatively recent decision by the Supreme Court of India in Appeal (Civil) No. 1859/2006 (State of Maharashtra v/s Sant Dhyaneshwar Shikshan Shastra Mahavidhyalaya Ors.) the following has been observed by the apex Court

"In fact, as held by this Court in cases referred to herein above, State Government has no power to reject the prayer of an institution or to overrule the decision of NCTE. The action of the State Government, therefore, was contrary to law and has rightly been set aside by the High Court."

It has also been stated in the above order that:

"It was also submitted that under the scheme of the Constitution, particularly Articles 245, 246, 248 and 254 read with Schedule VII thereof, only Parliament has power of co-ordination and determination of standards in institutions for higher education or research, scientific and technical institutions. State Legislatures have no authority to enact any law in the field covered by Entry 66 of List I of Schedule VII. Obviously, therefore, State Government has no authority to take a policy decision in respect of the subjects covered by Entry 66 of List I of Schedule VII for which a specific enactment has been made by Parliament and under the said Act authority has been granted to NCTE to take an action. As to Regulations and Guidelines, it was submitted that under the Act power has been conferred on NCTE. It is, therefore, only NCTE, which can consider the question and take appropriate decision under the Act and it is not open to NCTE to make Regulations or frame Guidelines empowering the State Government to undertake such exercise."

It would not be out of place to mention here that a few years back the NCTE on its official website (www.ncte-in.org) had earmarked a page eulogizing its regulatory and statutory status by giving the gist of the verdicts of the Supreme Court and various High Courts. Though that page is now not available, yet my computer's hard disk has that page still stored on it. The following gist of two such judgments is cited from that page:

Fixing a lower percentage of marks for admission than those prescribed by NCTE is contrary to law.

Maharshi Dayanand Saraswati University, Ajmer notifying that minimum eligibility criteria for admission to B.Ed. is 40% at Bachelors or Masters degree examination is a provision contrary to law. The Norms and Standards of NCTE having fixed 45% aggregate marks essential as admission criteria, fixation of a lower aggregate marks criteria is contrary to law, and is beyond the competence and outside the authority or power of the University. An advertisement issued (fixing a lower aggregate) would not act as estoppel against subsequently changing the criteria of marks which is in consonance with the norms and standards fixed by NCTE. (Rajasthan High Court)

(Order of the Hon'ble High Court of Rajasthan at Jodhpur dt. 9.9.97 Anop Singh Ratnu & Others Vs. MDS University, Ajmer).

Interpretation of eligibility criteria for B.Ed. Course under NCTE norms

There is nothing in the norms directing or stipulating that the minimum should only be 45%. On the other hand the norms (of NCTE) make it clear that for the purpose of B.Ed. Course, the minimum marks should be desirably 50% but not less than 45%. The Admission Rules, 1996 of the Govt. of Karnataka for B.Ed. Course prescribing a 50% (with a relaxation of 5% marks in the case of candidates belonging to SC/ST, category I of other Backward Community and physically handicapped persons) fulfils or achieves what the NCTE Norms require. The question of inconsistency or repugnancy would have arisen only if Norms had provided that the admission criteria shall not be more than 45% or provided that the minimum marks shall be 45%.

(Orders of the Hon'ble High Court of Karnataka at Bangalore dated 21.7.1997 in Writ Petitions Nos. 23722, 24105 to 24110/1996 etc. between certain institutions in Karnataka Vs. State of Karnataka and Others).

Now, the above detailed observations made by the judiciary about NCTE have deliberately been cited to create a background to contrast these with the following relevant excerpts from the Admission Notifications issued for B.Ed. Course in Rajasthan, Maharashtra and by the Indraprastha University, Delhi which show how the violation of the Norms enacted by the N.C.T.E. has taken place.

As per the Norms and Standards for Secondary Teacher Education program leading to Bachelor of Education (B.Ed.) Degree' published in the Gazette of India, Extraordinary, Part–III-Section A on July 21, 2006 the eligibility for doing B.Ed. is as follows:

"Candidates with at least 50% marks either in the Bachelor's Degree and/or in the Master's Degree or any other qualification equivalent thereto, are eligible for admission to the program."

In spite of this eligibility the Government of Rajasthan, the Government of Maharashtra, and the Indraprastha University, Delhi have come out with the eligibility conditions which are not in consonance with the above NCTE Norm and Standard.

In Rajasthan, only a B.A./B.Sc./B.Com or a Master's Degree holder with at least 50% marks with at least one school teaching subject has been considered eligible for filling up the form for admission in B.Ed. Thus many a graduate holding Bachelor's Degrees like that of B.C.A./B.B.A./B.Lib. /B.E / B.Tech. /B.Pharma., etc and the Master's degree holders like M.C.A., etc. have not even been allowed to fill in the admission forms.

The Indraprastha University, Delhi has clearly mentioned the following note in its Prospectus:

"However, the candidates having done B.Com.(Pass/ Hons.), Bachelor of Journalism (Mass Communication), BBA, BA (Vocational) are not eligible for the B.Ed. program. If a candidate having any of these degrees applies for Common Entrance Test for B.Ed. program, he or she will not be allowed to appear in the Test and if by default, he or she appears in the test, the admission will not be granted to such a candidate."

Apart from the above ineligibility the University also insists on having at least two school teaching subjects in one's Graduation. But Rajasthan insists that one school teaching subject is enough. The Government of Maharasthra in its admission notification has laid down the following admission criteria:

"The candidates who have obtained degree in Arts, Science, Commerce, Agricultural Science, Computer, Information Technology, Engineering and Home Science, B.S.W. from recognized University, Agricultural University, Open University and Deemed University and have completed their graduation/ post graduation with specialization in School or Higher Secondary Level Subject and have obtained minimum 45% marks in aggregate marks for OPEN, OBC and SBC candidate and 40% aggregate marks for Backward Class Candidates at degree/post graduate degree will be eligible for B.ED. CET Examination. Minimum marks criteria for outside Maharashtra candidates obtained criteria for all categories will be 45%."

From the above mentioned eligibility conditions as have been decided by different States it is revealed that none of these is as per the NCTE's Norms of 21st July 2006. While Rajasthan is not allowing all Bachelor's/Master's Degree holders, the Indraprastha University is also not allowing all of them; so much so that while Rajasthan and Maharashtra are allowing B.Com pass candidates the Indraprastha University is not even considering them eligible. While Rajasthan and the Indraprastha University insist on minimum 50% mark criteria; Maharashtra is satisfied with only 45%. The NCTE's Norm stipulates this figure to be at least 50%. So while one is eligible in Maharashtra he/she is not eligible in Rajasthan and the IP University, Delhi. Similarly, while one is eligible in Rajasthan and Maharashtra (B.Com. (Pass/Hons); he /she is ineligible in the I.P. University, Delhi. The crux of the situation is that all this variability exists in the presence of a Regulatory and Statutory Body framed by an Act of Parliament which mandates this Body under its Sec.12 as follows:

"It shall be the duty of the Council to take all such steps as it may think fit for ensuring planned and co-ordinated development of teacher education and for the determination and maintenance of standards for teacher education and for the purposes of performing its functions under this Act, the Council may .....–" and then are listed certain functions expected of the NCTE. A very pertinent function in the given context listed thereat in subsection (e) of Section 12 of the Act is to:

(e) lay down norms for any specified category of courses or trainings in teacher education, including the minimum eligibility criteria for admission thereof, and the method of selection of candidates, duration of the course, course contents and mode of curriculum;

It is not that this has happened for the first time. Way back in 2003 a CWP had been filed in the Hon'be Rajasthan High Court (CWP1805/2003 Arunima Jain v/s State & Ors.) on the ground that while B.Com. Graduates were not being allowed to be eligible for B.Ed. in Delhi, Kerala, Gujarat, and Tamilnadu they were being considered eligible in Rajasthan. Ms Arunima Jain raised the issue that if a B.Com. could not do B.Ed. in these four States how he or she could do the same in Rajasthan while the Norms and Standards as laid down by the NCTE were applicable all over the Country except J&K. This CWP was disposed off by the Hon'ble High Court of Rajasthan on 9th May 2003 with the following Order:

"The grievance as raised by the learned Counsel for the petitioner is that Jai Narain Vyas University which is conducting examinations for the entrance test of teachers training is not following the guidelines issued by the National Council for Teacher Education.

It would be advisable if the petitioner approaches NCTE itself, because NCTE is a statutory body having enough teeth to implement its policy. That being the position, no interference by this Court is called for.

Any representation made on behalf of the petitioner will be taken up by the NCTE and examined in right perspective. With these observations, the writ petition is disposed of."

Even after making representation to the NCTE the violation of the NCTE's Norm continued. Failing to find "enough teeth to implement its policy" in the mouth of the NCTE as had been believed by the Hon'ble High Court the petitioner Ms Arunima Jain moved a Contempt Writ Petition No. 56/2004. However, the contempt proceedings against the NCTE were dropped on 27th May 2004 on an assurance by the NCTE. The situations even then remained unchanged and the Government of Rajasthan continued the violation of the eligibility norms laid down by the NCTE. Constrained by such repeated violations Ms Arunima Jain again moved to the Hon'ble High Court with a CWP 1493/2004 (Arunima Jain v/s State & Ors.) which was disposed off on July 8, 2005 by the Hon'ble Mr Justice Prakash Tatia. Giving a very detailed Order the Hon'ble High Court passed many strictures against the working of the NCTE and also imposed a penalty of Rs. 25000/- (Rs. Twenty five thousand only) on the then Chairperson of the NCTE, New Delhi. The following direction to the NCTE was issued by the Hon'ble High Court: (perhaps this is the only Court Order best known to the author which indicted the role and performance of the NCTE and passed severe strictures against NCTE for its shabby style of working)

"that the commerce graduates shall be eligible for admission in B.Ed. Course for the current year only and the stay order granted by this Court on 25.02.2005 is vacated, the NCTE (apex body) is directed to consider and take steps to achieve the object for which the NCTE has been established by the National Council for Teacher Education Act, 1993 and prepare a plan to coordinate for development of the teacher education system throughout the country with the help of material and the consultations with the State Government authorities, Universities and educational institutions which may be relevant and help the NCTE to take an independent and considered plan for development of teachers education system for India and to avoid inconsistencies. The respondents NCTE is further directed to take a decision whether allowing the Commerce Graduates in B.Ed. Course in Rajasthan is required to be continued and if so whether Commerce Graduates in other States can be denied the same opportunities which are available to commerce students in Rajasthan? If it is permissible as per the norms of the NCTE, whether any step is needed or any corrections are needed and if needed then the NCTE may frame a scheme for parity of eligibility for different States. The decision about commerce graduates in the State of Rajasthan shall be taken by the NCTE at its highest level within a period of four months from the date of order so that dispute does not survive for the next year in the entrance examination."

Even after such a clear Order by the Hon'ble High Court neither the NCTE came out with any fresh or new directives in this regard nor could it curb the violation of its Norms in Rajasthan. The situation remained as it was prior to this Order. Consequently, Ms Arunima Jain was again constrained to file a new Contempt Writ Petition in the High Court of Rajasthan. Look at the plight of a girl who single handedly was fighting with three mighty organizations – the NCTE, the State Government, and the University conducting the Pre-Teacher Education Test (PTET) in Rajasthan. This was the Contempt Writ Petition during the hearing of which the then Chairperson of the NCTE presented himself before the Hon'ble High Court. The Contempt proceedings were dropped as he assured the Hon'ble High Court that the NCTE was coming out with fresh and revised Norms and Standards. The latest Norms and Standards of 21st July 2006 are the consequences of that assurance.

But even after the revised Eligibility conditions as laid down by the NCTE the situation remains unchanged. The violations are still continuing as presented above. The different States and Universities are blowing their own trumpets mutilating the Norms and Standards of the NCTE.

The violations are not only confined to Rajasthan, Maharashtra, and Indraprastha Univeristy, Delhi alone. Two other Central Universities in Delhi – University of Delhi and Jamia Millia Islamia – are also not allowing Graduates in Commerce (i.e. B.Com.) to do B.Ed. It would not be out of place to mention here that a Professor from the Department of Education, Jamia Millia Islamia, New Delhi is currently a member of the Northern Regional Committee (NRC) of the NCTE at Jaipur. He is there to oversee if the Norms and Standards of the NCTE for different Teacher Education programs are being adhered to by the teacher education institutions and Universities. It is ironic to note that his own University violates the Norms and Standards of the NCTE and he is neither able to prevent these violations nor able to prevent himself from being a member of the NRC, NCTE, Jaipur.

Two other States are also there who have allowed the Graduates/Post Graduates with only 45% as eligible for doing B.Ed. These States are – Haryana and Andhra Pradesh.

These dichotomies in the Eligibility conditions are not the solitary instances of the violations of the NCTE Norms and Standards. Other violations also persist and continue unabated.

The Section 4.4 (d) (Terms and Conditions of service) of the Norms and Standards notified on 21st July 2006 stipulates as follows:

"The academic staff of the institutions (including part-time staff) shall be paid such salary in such scale of pay as may be prescribed by the UGC/University from time to time, through an account payee cheque or as per advice into the bank account of employee specially opened for the purpose. The supporting staff shall be paid as per the UGC/State Government/Central Government pay scale structure."

In spite of such a clear directive the teachers in the Teachers' Colleges in Rajasthan teaching for B.Ed., M.Ed. and Ph.D. (Education) are getting the salary in the scale of pay of Government School teachers and not "getting the salary in the scale of pay as may be prescribed by the UGC/University from time to time."

To continue further, the Department of Education, University of Rajasthan, Jaipur where M.Ed. course is offered there are only two teachers working on the full time and regular basis against the requirement of 5 teachers as stipulated under the NCTE's Norms and Standards for M.Ed. program. It should not be out of place to mention here that the Regional Director, Northern Regional Committee, NCTE has its office in Jaipur itself and such a violation is taking place under his very nose.

It is not that the NCTE is oblivious of these violations. A number of letters in the form representations have been sent to the NCTE HQ as well as to its Regional Office. What to talk of anybody else Sh. Rajeev Kumar, IAS – Secretary Education, Govt of Uttar Pradesh stated in one of the meetings of the NRC that existing B. Ed. colleges are not following the guidelines of the State Government/UGC for the admission of students, which they have to follow as per article 3.3 of NCTE Regulations dated 20th July 2006 (Norms for Secondary teacher education program). The minutes of the said meeting are available on http://www.ncte-in.org/nrc/minutes/Min116th-II.pdf

Every violation of any Norm framed by a regulatory and statutory body is usually considered a very serious offence. It ought to be more so, when it relates to the minimum eligibility of doing a University Degree program. Any University Degree is recognized nationally and even internationally. A Degree obtained in Maharashtra fetches a job for the Degree holder all over the Country.

It is therefore lies in nobody's mouth to tell the world that ".... Quality of teacher education can only be effectively ensured by NCTE, only when the State governments are willing to do so. In a federal set up, it is not desirable that the central statutory body will adopt legal steps to compel States to stick to certain guidelines. Hence, the State Governments are to be blamed for the dilution of teacher training, not the NCTE." (Mohanty, Sunil Behary in Appraisal of Performance of a Decade of Functioning of National Council for Teacher Education, pp. 5-6 University News, 45(33), August 13-19, 2007)

The NCTE is adequately equipped by the Parliament of India to get its Norms implemented all over the Country except J&K. If the violations still take place and the NCTE remains a silent watcher the reasons may be different. Naturally, it requires tons of moral courage to take action against the defaulters.

The Norms and Standards of the NCTE fall into the category of Subordinate Legislation and every Norm is referred to the Committees on Subordinate Legislation in the Lok Sabha and the Rajya Sabha. The NCTE by not ensuring one hundred percent compliance and adherence to by all the stakeholders to its Norms in fact is also misleading the Parliament of India and thus the whole Nation. These issues have already reached the notice of the Chairmen of the Subordinate Legislation Committees both in the Lok Sabha and the Rajya Sabha.

Now, have a look at another facet of the working of the NCTE. A recent phenomenon is the opening of M.A. Education course by a number of Universities and colleges. This presents the flip side of the teacher education system in the country. While the NCTE prescribes M.A. Education as a qualification acceptable for becoming a Lecturer in a Teacher Education College, it has not made any Norms for this program. If it is a Teacher Education program it cannot remain outside the purview of the NCTE; and if it is not a teacher education program it cannot be a qualification for becoming a teacher educator. If M.A. Education can be an alternative qualification to a M.Ed. the question arises is: Is B.A. Education equivalent to B.Ed.? I put this question to the NCTE HQ under Right to Information and got flak from the NCTE.

I request the readers to explain the differences between these two Degrees. Suffice to say that Vardhman Mahaveer Kota Open University, Kota (Rajasthan) and some more institutions have already started M.A. Education with an unlimited number of seats. Can the NCTE check up this mass production of M.A. Education candidates? And also explain; to what end they are being prepared?

I asked the Public Information Officer (PIO) of the NCTE, Delhi as to how no Norms have been prepared for M.A. Education programme. Vide his office letter no. F.109 31/2007/NCTE/CDN/ 64929 dated April 16, 2007 the following was conveyed to me:

"As per Section 2(m) of the NCTE Act, teacher education qualification means a qualification in teacher education (as defined in section 2(l) of the Act) which equip a person to teach at pre-primary, primary, secondary and senior secondary stages in schools etc. As such M.A. (Edn) is not covered under this definition."

What a bizarre reply and situation! If as per Section 2(m) of the NCTE Act 1993, the teacher education qualification means a qualification in teacher education (as defined in Section 2(l) of the Act) which equips a person to teach at pre-primary, primary, secondary and senior secondary stages in schools and since M.A. Education is not a qualification which equips someone to teach at any of these stages then the question arises: Does an M.Ed. degree equip someone to teach at any of these stages? M.Ed. too does not equip anyone to teach at any of these stages and yet the NCTE has framed Norms for it and no institution can start M.Ed. program without the permission of the NCTE.

If the provisions of the Section 2(m) of the NCTE Act 1993 are correctly read it will be apparent that M.Ed. is not a teacher education qualification and the NCTE had no business to frame any Norms and Standards for this Course or program. By the same logic if M.A. (Education) cannot come within the purview of the NCTE, M.Ed. too cannot remain within its purview.

Another issue is that if M.A. Education is equivalent to M.Ed. then logically B.A. Education must also be equivalent to B.Ed. Why is it then not so? The NCTE as an apex body needs to answer this query.

The Norms are never cosmetic in nature; they serve no purpose if they are only to be published in the official gazette and then put on the official web site of the NCTE. They serve the real purpose only when they are implemented in soul and spirit. If they are consistently violated and there is no mechanism to prevent such violations then they remain cosmetic in nature and with the NCTE around they currently appear to be so. And it is not a new or recent phenomenon. Moreover, there have been Norms which were prepared, then amended, and then amended again to bring them back to the original provision This puts the wisdom of the NCTE under a scanner. This also shows that the NCTE has been such an institution where the Norms can be amended at the whims and fancy of anyone on any day. The following is the illustration of one such Norm.

The NCTE's Norm for the salary structure of the teacher-educators, in 1996 stated:

"The institution should adopt the salary structure prescribed by the U.G.C./Central/State Govt as the case may be for its teaching and non-teaching staff."

Then in the year 1997 vide The Gazette of India, Notification No. 29 of July 19, 1997 (Application for recognition, the manner for submission, determination of conditions for recognition of institutions and permission to start new course or training (Amendment)) the NCTE amended its existing Norm and it was replaced by the following which stated under the heading, "Nature of Employment of Staff":

"All staff shall be appointed on full time and regular basis, after selection by a duly constituted Selection Committee. The salary structure for teaching staff shall be as per UGC Norms."

This Norm of the NCTE remained in force till March 27, 1999 when it was again amended vide The Gazette of India No. 13 of March 23, 1999 and the things were made what they were prior to 1997 amendment i.e. the Salary Structure for the teaching staff shall be as per the UGC/Central/State Govt.

These amendments present a very peculiar aspect of NCTE's working. The Norm for the UGC pay scales to the teaching staff of the Secondary Teacher-education institutes remained in force for almost two years i.e. from July 19, 1997 to March 27, 1999 but the teachers working in Teachers' Colleges in Rajasthan did never have and still do not have the UGC pay-scales. Now the pertinent question is that what the NCTE was doing to see whether its Norm was being implemented by the State Governments concerned or not. How come this Norm went unimplemented by the State Government concerned?

When Norms are prepared, I believe a lot of thinking goes into these and the amendments are always necessitated to accommodate prevailing circumstances. One would like to know what circumstances had forced the NCTE to make amendments initially once and then came the re-amendments as mentioned above? How come this feeling lasted two years and then suddenly it underwent transformation? Looks as though the earlier wisdom got hijacked by the earlier one and the subsequent Norm was amended again. If the NCTE had any mechanism to see that its Norms were implemented by the parties concerned the teacher-educators of Rajasthan and would have been getting the UGC pay scales today. Alas! It never happened. The latest Norm of 21 July 2006 continues to remain unimplemented in this regard in Rajasthan and the NCTE remains unmoved.

The University Grants Commission (UGC) implemented the recommendations of Mungekar Committee and vide its Notification F.No.1-1/2002(PS) Exemp. 14th June, 2006 the following provision was notified:

"NET shall remain the compulsory requirement for appointment as Lecturer for those with post-graduate degree. However, the candidates having Ph.D. degree in the concerned subject are exempted from NET for PG level and UG level teaching. The candidates having M.Phil degree in the concerned subject are exempted from NET for UG level teaching only."

Contrast the above qualification requirements with what NCTE promulgated on 21 July 2006 in the Gazette of India Extraordinary Part - III Section-4:

"..............the candidates shall have to qualify NET/SLET qualifications or alternative qualifications thereto as prescribed by UGC from time to time before the commencement of the academic session 2009-2010."

The Times of India (July 10, 2006) on its page 11 i.e. TIMES NATION carried a Notification issued by Maharshi Valmiki College of Education, Geeta Colony, Delhi-31. It is a College of the Govt. of NCT of Delhi. This Notification in fact was a corrigendum in the qualifications announced earlier for the posts of Lecturer in Education (Methods of Teaching Hindi, Economics, Physics, Chemistry, History, Sanskrit) and had been issued in the light of the new or revised qualifications as announced by the UGC in its Notification of 14th June 2006 Read below the Notification from the TOI.

"Reference Advertisement dated 31.03.06 in daily "Times of India" for six different posts of Lecturer in Education (Methods of Teaching Hindi, Economics, Physics, Chemistry, History, and

Sanskrit)."NET shall remain the compulsory requirement for appointment as Lecturer for those with Post-graduate degree. However, the candidates having Ph.D. Degree in the concerned subject are exempted from NET for PG level and UG level teaching. The candidates having M.Phil. Degree in the concerned subject are exempted from NET for UG level teaching only." Those who have not applied earlier may do so within seven (7) days of the publication of this notice."

Now, this Notification is violative of the Norm laid down by the National Council for Teacher Education (NCTE) but is in consonance with the UGC Notification. One is eligible as per the NCTE norm but is not eligible as per the UGC regulation. The NCTE Norm says that only a PG Degree in Education will suffice to become eligible for the post of a Lecturer in a Teacher Education college while the UGC regulation says otherwise.

The question is: Was the College correct if it acted upon the UGC Notification and not upon the NCTE Norm? Can such dichotomies be allowed between the eligibility qualifications of two Statutory and Regulatory bodies both framed by the Acts of Parliament? Do the Universities have no qualms if the University Degrees are awarded to such students whose teachers are neither Ph.D. nor M.Phil.? and; who are also not NET qualified in Education? What would happen to the verdict of the Supreme Court in the famous PIL filed by Prof. Yashpal in the matter of the private Universities of Chattisgarh when it pronounced that the "minimum levels of instruction" must be fulfilled before the grant of any University Degree? Don't the qualifications of the teachers teaching for University Degrees affect the "minimum levels of instruction"?

Another big question is that even if this dichotomy is allowed to survive how before 21 July 2006 the NCTE, the Universities, the Colleges, and the State Governments allowed non NET/SLET qualified and non-M.Phil and non-Ph.D. individuals to get appointed in the B.Ed. Colleges?

At least in Rajasthan none of these qualifications was ever required to become a teacher in any University affiliated Teachers' College. And since the exemption in these qualifications was granted only on 21 July 2006 it clearly shows that till 20 July 2006 these were the essential qualifications. Were these qualifications ever adhered to? The reply is big NO And the NCTE knew this fully well and knew it even in the year 1998.

The NCTE's document No, 98/18 (State Studies on Teacher Education: Teacher Education in Rajasthan) contains the following information.

On page no. 65 of this document under the heading 'Recruitment of Teacher Educators of Government Institutions' the following documented statements are written:

"As stated earlier, there are no separate policy documents, cadres and service rules for teacher educators of government institutions. Academic staff of schools and teacher education institutions is inter-transferable. Primarily, academic staff is required for school for different grades and out of these suitable staff is posted in teacher education institutions. Normally, academic staff with an M.Ed. degree is identified for these institutions. No separate cadre is created for the staff of teacher education institutions....."

The above admission by the NCTE in its own document is sufficient enough that exemption from Ph.D., M.Ed., and NET was always available at least in Rajasthan while it officially granted this exemption only on 21 July 2006. This is sufficient to reveal that the NCTE was never very serious about the qualifications and the service conditions of the teachers in the Teachers' Colleges nor did the UGC and the Universities ever cared for such violations which were eating into the roots of the teacher education in the country.

In the same document inn Appendix 2 (list and addresses of Institutions) (on page no. 167) the name of Shri Shikshram Ola has been shown as the Head of Institution of I.B.B.N. B.Ed. College, Ardawata, Jhunjhunu. Was Mr. Ola who presently is a Cabinet Minister in the Central Government ever a Principal of a B.Ed. College? The NCTE says it so and that too in its published document.

On page no. 56 (Chapter 5 – Management of Teacher Education) under the 'Rules for Affiliation' the said document mentions certain rules for affiliation of Teachers' Colleges. One of them is as follows:

"Each academic staff member will have minimum qualifications prescribed by the university and will be paid salary according to university norms."

On page no. 58 of the same Chapter the following documented fact under the heading 'Staff' is available:

The staff should be duly qualified in accordance with the minimum qualifications and on minimum emoluments laid down by the university from time to time."

The question is: Were these provisions ever followed?

Now, we must turn to another very significant aspect that deals with the basic structure of school education vis-à-vis the teacher education. This apex and expert body has not been able to decide very basic and fundamental issues. Is B.Ed. a general degree enabling someone to teach any subject under the sky or is it a subject specific degree? Are the methodologies of teaching subject specific? Can a teacher trained or educated to teach Science subjects be allowed to teach Social Sciences or languages? If it is so then on what logic the thousands of students are not being allowed to do B.Ed. on the pretext that they do not have the school teaching subject in their graduation? Why is a B. Com then not being allowed to do B.Ed. by any Universities in Delhi?

The picture of the supervision of practice teaching lessons presents a gloomy scene. The teachers of Science are found supervising lessons of languages including Sanskrit and of Social Sciences; the teachers of languages and Social Sciences supervise those of Sciences. The entire teacher education system is in doldrums. How does one answer D.S. Kothari who believed that the destiny of the Nation was made in its classrooms?

Read the following that has come from Uganda and see for yourself how close our teacher education system is to a seemingly educationally struggling country.

"A student has been quoted saying, " It is not surprising for a Luganda lecturer to supervise a History class".

Musimenta, a student of Kyambogo University says, "I had never seen the people who turned up to supervise me. I had anticipated lecturers but they did not turn up." Musimenta believes supervisors can be more effective if they have good knowledge of the subject matter.

Kaigwa, a Makerere student of Economics and History, shares a similar view. Kaigwa, who is doing his School Practice (SP) at Bukhooli College in Bugiri, says he has been supervised two times and none of the supervisors was his lecturer."

A wonderful advice for us comes from Muwe[illegible]do who says, "If a lecturer who is well-versed with the subject supervises a student, they h/she can give them guidelines on how to deliver content to the learners in a better way."

A lecturer at Kyambogo University says that sometimes the universities underpay the supervisors, which kills their morale." (All these details have been taken from 'Uganda: Are Student Teachers Benefiting from School Practice? by Luke Kagiri, Mary Karugaba and George Bita of Kampala – http://allafrica.com/stories/200707300068.html)

The entire Sarva Shiksha Abhiyan (SSA), a flagship program of the present UPA Government, is based on the premise that the Elementary Education is the education of children between 6-14 years of age studying in classes 1 to 8. Then how is that the teachers having Elementary teacher education qualification (like JBT, D.Ed., BSTC, PTC, etc) are not being allowed to teach classes 6 to 8? How are the teachers having the degree of B.Ed. which is a Secondary Teacher Education qualification being allowed to teach the classes 6 to 8 which fall into the category of Elementary Education? It is ironical that the Norms of the NCTE for the qualifications of teachers for different levels of schools do not make any distinctions between the Elementary school teacher education qualifications and the Secondary school teacher education qualifications. It is altogether a different issue if the NCTE is competent enough to lay down qualifications for the school teachers as the school education falls into the domain of the State List and not the Centre List.

Prof J. S. Rajput in his paper says : "Bringing about the desired level of quality in teacher education and developing and enforcing norms and standards is a difficult and challenging task, especially in a country of India's size and diverse conditions, with regard to material, manpower and infrastructure, and limited financial resources."

I would only like to dwell upon the aspect of "limited financial resources". Shruti Maheshwari in 'Gurus Get It all Wrong' (India Today, July 23, 2007 p. no. 51-52) says: "The sum collected as application fee (NCTE received almost 4000 applications every year with each applicant paying Rs. 40,000 which means a minimum earning of Rs. 16 crore every year) is kept in a current account with no planning of expected income and expenditure or investment."

The Chapter 12 of mandatory disclosures made under the RTI Act 2005 by the NCTE and available on http://www.ncte-in.org/rti/index.htm gives a figure of Rs. 998.59 lacs as the Budget estimates of NCTE for the year 2005-06. The expenditure of NCTE during 2004-05 has been shown as under:

Figures in Rs.

H.Q.	*NRC*	*WRC*	*SRC*	*ERC*
65821845.14	9570445.00	7082125.00	1704155.00	9609315.00

Note: The figures given above are exclusive of remittances made to/from HQ/Regional Committees.

From the above Table, the total expenditure of the NCTE comes out to Rs. 109025280.14 for a single financial year which is quite a huge figure and still the talk of limited financial resources is heard.

I am nobody to pass any judgment on the issue whether the NCTE must remain or go. Let the Parliament of India decide on this issue in its sagacity and wisdom. However, the Nation needs answers to the following questions:

1. Is there no alternative left with the Government but to close the NCTE down by repealing the Act? I feel that

competent and able people with impeccable integrity and honesty are still available who can handle the affairs of the Teacher Education in the Country.

2. A White Paper on the functioning of the NCTE since its inception needs to be immediately brought out so that the Nation knows as to what happened in and to the NCTE so that Mr Banerjee Committee now has to recommend such an extreme step as solution.

3. How can the personnel involved with the functioning (or the malfunctioning) of the NCTE be allowed to go scot free without being accountable and answerable to the Nation if their non-performance has brought the things to such a pass that now the closure is the only remedy available?

4. The NCTE Act was enacted in 1993 to "maintain and coordinate the standards of the teacher education in the country". Prior to that it were the Universities that were overlooking the Degree level teacher education in the country. Certainly, the things at that time were not quite satisfactory and the teacher education faced problems. Does the MHRD now feel that the UGC and the Universities are functioning quite satisfactorily and handing over the affairs of the Teacher Education to the Universities will resolve all problems?

5. A very big part of the Teacher Education which relates to the Certificate and the Diploma Courses in the Teacher Education (like JBT, D.Ed., C.PEd, etc) does not come within the purview of the Universities. Who'll regulate this very big part of the Teacher Education? Or, will it go unregulated? It is therefore urgently felt that before the decision of the closure of the NCTE is taken the above issues must be answered in right earnest.

I wish the NCTE to always recall the following reverberating words of Hon'ble Justice Mr Prakash Tatia of Rajasthan High Court which he used while delivering judgment in CWP No. 1293/2004 (Arunima Jain vs State & Ors.) on July 8, 2005.

"More shocking is that the same norms and standards prescribed by the NCTE are interpreted by the different States and Union Territories to deny admission to the commerce graduates in B.Ed. courses but are interpreted in the State of Rajasthan to permit commerce graduates to take admission in B.Ed. and seek appointment." (para 31)

"There is no hesitation in holding that there is force in the contention of the learned counsel for the petitioner that the norms which are laid down by the NCTE are binding upon all the States and the standards fixed by the NCTE cannot be lowered down, what to say of Colleges, Universities but even by the State." (para 40)

"The NCTE failed to explain reason for laying down the norms which according to the NCTE itself can be interpreted by the State as per their alleged policies which may destroy the entire aim and object of enacting the NCTE Act, 1993 and which may allow disparities in standard of teacher education." (para 47), and finally

"Therefore, the writ petition of the petition is partly allowed with a direction to the respondent NCTE (a) to overhaul their own working first before overhauling system of teacher education."

A word to UGC is also essential here. There should not be any dichotomies between the Regulations framed by it and by the NCTE. These two regulatory bodies must work in tandem as both have identical aims to maintain and coordinate the standards of higher education in the country.

After all the above discussion it is now the time when Yeats and Shelley both come to mind together. While Yeats says

Things fall apart; the centre cannot hold;

Mere anarchy is loosed upon the world,

Shelley is always there to remind us:

"If Winter comes, can Spring be far behind?"

Hopefully, after the terrible winters the teacher education in the country had to live with a day will surely come when Spring will be around.

* Contact *Lecturer, S.G.K. Teachers' College (C.T.E.)

Jodhpur- 342003 (Rajasthan)

E: mail drjite@gmail.com

SECTION - IV

12

Teaching Teachers for a Knowledge Society

R.P.SINGH

"To remain human and livable knowledge societies will have to be societies of shared knowledge. The plural here sanctions the need for an accepted diversity….. There has been much reference to the digital divide, which is a reality. But a still more disturbing factor is that the knowledge divide between the most favored and the developing countries, particularly the least developed is liable to widen while, within societies themselves, equally profound cleavages appear or are exacerbated. How could the future societies settle for the future being 'dissociated societies"?
"Koichiro Matsuura, Director General, UNESCO, **Towards Knowledge Societies**, 2002

The solution to the problems raised in the above quote lies in preparing for better education in the classrooms. Since it is the teachers who matter in the classrooms our attention should be focused on them. It is not enough to give directions to the teachers for how to conduct themselves in the classrooms, it is imperative that their role is clearly understood and accepted by

those who are responsible for their training and education. Unfortunately, we seem to have failed at this stage. The universities that should have been in the vanguard as torch-bearers and the NCTE whose primary concern should have been to improve the health of teacher preparation are themselves in need of extra medication. India's National Knowledge Commission (**NKC**) set up under the chairmanship of Sam Pitroda (perhaps inspired by the UNESCO Report cited above) is currently holding nation-wide discussions on the direction it must take. The present paper is a small contribution in that direction.

I personally regard that a proper resolution to all socio-economic problems generally emanates from the educational system. Since this system is manned by the teachers, in the final analysis the answers must also come from them.

The present paper is focused on the ensuing questions. 1. What exactly do we mean by a 'knowledge society'? What would be its nature? 2. How can the teachers contribute to make that society vibrant and livable? And 3.What happens to the diversity / and, the digital divide – the class structure and the question of homogeneity? Additionally, what would be the real curriculum like?

I have tried to deal with each aspect of the questions raised.

The Nature of Knowledge Society

The term knowledge society was first mentioned by Peter Drucker in 1969 but it came into its own in the 1990's. Earlier on R.M. Hutchins' (in the 1950's) had talked of 'Information' societies. For him too the degree of educational accessibility was one of the measures of achieving that goal even as for becoming knowledge society common and wide access to education remain the only measures of achievement. Of course the 'quality' matters and so do the goals of which primarily the principle that governs the attainment is the common accessibility. It is about the same time two more concepts took birth. While the one was the notion of 'learning' societies, the other one was 'Lifelong' education. Even otherwise humans continue to learn throughout their life time, irrespective of the claims a few make that at a given age an individual's learning stops.

Today the concept of knowledge society has become an essential framework of reflection not only for the member countries of the OECD but also for developing economies and nations.

The Commission however makes one thing quite clear. Knowledge societies are not new or of recent origin. Only their definitions have not remained constant. Historically, all societies have been knowledge societies but their models were different. In essence older societies were class-based with little or no communication of intellectual achievements with the masses. Socrates had his audience, even as Kant had his. Their concerns did not percolate down to the common man. Until then the concept of 'common' man itself had not taken birth. In reality, the common man himself is a 20th century product although the ground had been made fallow by the Renaissance and the Age of Enlightenment and the terminal conditions of the medieval age.

The Age of *free and compulsory* education even in the advanced societies had not dawned until the middle of 20th century. Therefore, it is not surprising that *secular* education itself took a long time getting freed from the clutches of the priestly classes. A few societies that have not as yet known the concept of "free, compulsory and non-priestly or secular" education are going to take some more time to emerge out of the dark ages, where superstition and divinity are indistinguishable. But that is past. In the new age under the guidance of UNESCO, we could enter the New Era, and indeed we have.

The UNESCO document defines the future knowledge societies. "*A knowledge society should be able to integrate all its members and to promote new forms of solidarity involving both present and future generations. Nobody should be excluded from knowledge societies,* ***where knowledge is a public good, available to each and every individual.*"** p.18

It goes on to distinguish the present and the future societies from the older societies stating, "Since the 'information age' knowledge societies differ from older knowledge societies because of the focus of human rights and the participatory behavior they inherited from the Enlightenment, the importance of basic rights translates into the particular emphasis on; (1) freedom of opinion and expression," (Article 19of the Universal Declaration of Human Rights), (2) the right to education and its corollary, free basic education and progress towards free access to other levels of education, (Article 26, of the Universal Declaration of Human Rights) and, (3) the right 'freely to participate in the cultural life of the community, to enjoy the arts and share in scientific advancement and its benefits (Article 27, Paragraph. 1, of the Universal Declaration of Human Rights)

In the new age technology and education have got so integrated that one cannot think of one without the other. On all hands, we acknowledge that youth is ever so willing to change and it has currently taken to the use of technology even as the duck takes to water. The problem is that teachers—the most conservative elements, are being forced to take cognizance of the changes occurring all around them. While the world has been won over by the communication technology, its use in the classrooms has been quite slow. The cause does not lie in the cost alone, but in the mindset also. We have to create conditions that this scenario also changes radically. Once this happens and the nature and the text of classrooms undergoes a radical change half the battle will have been won.

The New Classrooms—Functions and Goals

We must remember that once the demands of the classrooms change, willy-nilly the teachers will also change. Advanced countries are already using these technologies and accordingly we in India too must also start using them extensively. Initially cost may be a factor in its use but once we have put the technologies in place, as a clever nation we shall not face many difficulties. Let us recount the way the new technologies have impacted knowledge societies. "In emerging knowledge societies, there is also a virtuous circle in which the progress of knowledge and technological innovation produces more knowledge in the long term. We are witnessing an acceleration of knowledge production. The new technology marks the entrance of information and knowledge in a cumulative logic, which Manuel Castells describes as 'the application of such knowledge to knowledge generation and information processing / communication devices, in a cumulative feedback loop between an innovation and the uses of innovation.'

The new technologies have brought in their train new values and the new avenues for the creation and sustenance of new knowledge societies. What characterizes the Knowledge Societies are creativity and innovation. Creativity and innovations have led to the formation of new types of collaborative processes. It is here that societies have to evolve methods to achieve the heightened and enriched goals. Clearly the goals of education cannot ignore the reality. The reality is that that both creativity and innovations have been the twin cherished values and therefore they have continued to be nurtured in all 'free' and 'progressive' societies. While the autocratic and 'closed' societies look upon these values as a threat to their existence, (see, Karl Popper; The 'Open' Society an its Enemies), the 'open' societies welcome them.

The UNESCO report underscores the fact that despite the advent of global information society we have as yet to become a knowledge society in the real sense of the term. The real reason behind it all is that large masses are deprived of access to education, which to say the least is not only due to gender bias, but also due to appalling levels of poverty. Without access to education information will never be anything but 'a mass of indistinct data' because where else could one learn to master the available information with critical judgment and the thinking and to analyze, sort and incorporate the items they consider interesting in a knowledge base.

The said report warns against regarding excess information necessarily as the source of additional knowledge. The idea is that an individual should be able to distinguish between 'useful' and 'useless; information and this is virtually impossible, if one has not developed cognitive and critical skills. 'Useful' information does not always yield itself to profitable ends and one should remember that humanist and scientific knowledge have differing goals and functions. 'Making the most of knowledge to imagining a new and collaborative development model based on the guarantee by the government of 'public property', where growth is no longer viewed as an end in itself, but simply as a means of reaching the target.

The aim of being a knowledge society is to have empirically verifiable 'freedom' for all and not to have just a Right to this or that. The idea is to have equal access to information and the right to collective security. Network societies as knowledge societies are necessarily aware of global concerns. For instance knowledge is a potent tool in the fight against those who are opposed to knowledge societies. The successes achieved in this direction have largely been the result of massive investments in education. It is the realization that mere connectivity or networking is not enough unless people are made to acquire skills of reflections and logic. One must remember that commoditization of knowledge is as harmful a development as the uniformity in the thought processes is. *Diversity of cognitive cultures remains the cherished goal of a knowledge society.* After all knowledge, thought and conscience constitute the dignity of human beings. If schools and education for all are essential for acquiring knowledge, skills in reflection and communication remain the basic functions of an educational system. "In the absence of 'freedom of expression' knowledge may still exist, however, there can be no knowledge society or any knowledge sharing." (Report, p. 20)

The goals of education for a knowledge society are to train students to reflect, make them logical, help them in learning to communicate, assist them to be creative and enable them in innovations while making them feel free to be different from others. The function and purpose of the new classrooms are to achieve precisely all these objectives. By making available basic tools for learning networking and easy access to education are imperative.

Teaching Teachers for a Knowledge Society

Having defined the purpose and the ends of education for a knowledge society all that needs to be discussed briefly is the outline of a teacher training program. It is imperative that we discuss the initial teacher education first. Implied in this statement is the fact that no one can devise a training program that would enable its recipient to remain in step with the changing times. Educational system is generally regarded as the most conservative element in an otherwise dynamic society. We have thus to be extra careful in suggesting novel ideas. We must devise both short term and long term goals. Therefore, one should think of a program that makes one fit enough for a short duration – say, for the first five years. The rest would depend on the changing needs and requirements of a given Time and Society. We have to have two types of teacher education programs –one, short term i.e. one or more years' program and the life-long. ("Lifelong education thus entails transforming and re-harmonizing individuals and social periods of learning. Over a lifespan, several periods of education and training can be identified.") Jacques Delors in his report titled ***Learning To Be*** made a proposal in the form of "study-time entitlement." for life-long learning

The *initial training program* should however focus on:

1. Making students creative / and, innovative. In place of expecting them to repeat what is given they may be encouraged to suggest alternatives that enable them to reach their goals early. The ritual of instruction in which memorization plays a big role has to be given a go-by. ("Even though we usually stress the tendency toward dematerialization taking place in network societies, the new technologies have also enabled us to materialize and externalize various cognitive functions thanks to machines") It is therefore noteworthy that in the 'information revolution' the new artifacts and new types of information quickly become commonplace. To remain competitive one has always to remain on the tenterhooks. Hence, there is the need to be continuously innovative and creative.

2. In the knowledge societies one could notice easily the changes taking place in the process of access to knowledge. Compared with the knowledge societies the present educational system continues to be conservative and is also heavily dependent on the print and verbal instruction. The advances already made available via developments in information and communication technology have not been accepted by the conservative elements with open arms. This situation needs rectification.

3. Teaching could be conducted through dialogue, discussion and question-answer sessions where students are free to be inquisitive and creative. The key lies in the 'freedom' which enables a dialogue to become meaningful. It is noteworthy that 'good' teachers so encourage their students that they are happy to learn new things and welcome the students who suggest new ideas. Youth has ideas. They are ever willing to experiment. Ideas need to be given shape. They need to be tried. All progress can be ascribed to reflection and the trial of new ideas. It is not easy but that should be the goal of good education.

4. While Creativity and Innovations are the twin ideals for achievement, *logic constitutes the base for all discussions.* We have reached a point where the aims of education have to be redefined. The UNESCO report says," the most thought-provoking vision for the future of education is the constitution of new humanities to occupy the void gradually left by outdated literary traditions, to bridge the gap between scientific knowledge and the human sciences, and to provide a synoptic grasp of current knowledge... if a field of study is not just to be an accumulation of facts, a dead letter, it is vital for learners to know where the knowledge they are required to learn comes from and how it was developed. How do the scientists work? The magnitude of these challenges for

education calls for trained teaching staff with updated knowledge about the latest technological, scientific and epistemological development both in their own subject area and in the educational processes themselves." (P.80)

5. In the knowledge societies students are not perceived as passive listeners. The model, which teaches how to solve problems instead of offering ready-made solutions, confronts students with didactic situations, in which there is an obstacle to be overcome. Problem solving combines practical experimentation with theoretical knowledge in order to arouse the imagination and stimulate motivation.

6. Both for making the young conscious of the large number of biases our society suffers from such as gender, color and caste biases besides the tribal and the non-tribal ones. These biases are not easy to overcome. A deliberate attempt has to be made to understand the nature of these biases and evolve methods for overcoming them.

In the end, it is the function of the governments to help, and create conditions to enable a society transform itself. The private and the corporate sectors may also be welcomed to make their contribution. But this does not mean that the governments could shun away from shouldering their main roles of guiding and supervising the overall functioning and the direction of the system. After all, teachers have to conjure up a vision and the students have to give it a shape but this cannot become a reality without the guidance of the government and the willing acceptance of the society as a whole.

* Formerly with the NCERT, currently **President, All India Association of Teacher Educators,** E:-mail profrpsi@gmail.com tel. 2603062 Residence Pocket A-4, Kalkaji Ext. New Delhi —110019

Index

C

Q

R

W

Y